ADVANCE PRAISE

"This is an exhilarating read. The author masterfully captures the harrowing journey of his parents, tracing their struggles and triumphs before, during, and after the war. Willie's meticulous historical research weaves together these stories, offering profound insight into the enduring strength and vulnerabilities of the human spirit. Unflinching clarity reveals the unimaginable horrors and the incredible resilience that defines the lives of his family and his experiences being a child of survivors. The issues are explored with deep empathy, highlighting the complex legacy of trauma and survival. Be prepared for the haunting echoes from the past on the present reality of the rise of antisemitism and Holocaust denial."

–Jenni Frumer, PhD, LCSW, MSEd, Director, NOW for Holocaust Survivors Initiative/MorseLife Health System.

"Sharing where we come from and who we are is difficult. In *Out from the Shadows*, Willie Handler does just that, he exposes himself as part of a minority which historically has been blamed and hated for millennia. Releasing his memoir is both brave, and a strong move that is dedicated to helping save the world from it's own hatred. People can evolve as human beings, if they read and educate themselves. This book helps assist the reader in understanding and believing the history, and taking a look inward to recognize personal biases."

–Karen Zauder Brass, Founder of the anti-bullying movement Standupsters, International Speaker, and author of *Trauma Filters Through, I Am A Standupster*, and the children's book, *How To Create Peace. Teaching Children To Navigate Their Personal Choices.*"

OUT FROM THE SHADOWS

GROWING UP WITH HOLOCAUST SURVIVOR PARENTS

WILLIE HANDLER

ISBN 9789493322905 (ebook)

ISBN 9789493322882 (paperback)

ISBN 9789493322899 (hardcover)

Publisher: Amsterdam Publishers, The Netherlands

info@amsterdampublishers.com

Out from the Shadows is part of the series Holocaust Heritage

Copyright © Willie Handler 2024

Cover image: Willie Handler's Grandparents' apartment in Bedzin

All Rights Reserved. No part of this publication may be reproduced or transmitted in any form or by any means, electronic or mechanical, including photocopy, recording or any other information storage and retrieval system, without prior permission in writing from the publisher.

CONTENTS

Foreword   ix
Family Trees   xiii

1. Prewar Bedzin   1
2. Prewar Comanesti   7
3. Bedzin Ghetto   12
4. Forced Labor Camps   16
5. The Kamionka Ghetto   19
6. Extermination through Work   24
7. Expulsion from Comanesti   28
8. Trading Shoes for Food   31
9. Destruction of the Jews of Bedzin   34
10. Dad's First Family   38
11. Sonderkommando   41
12. Angel of Death   44
13. Resilience and Resistance   47
14. Oksenhendler Family Survivors   53
15. Zloczower Family Survivors   57
16. Liberation and the Aftermath   60
17. An Eye for An Eye   64
18. New Life in Israel   67
19. Walking the Streets of Bedzin   73
20. Trauma and Memory   83
21. Who names a Child Willie Handler?   92
22. My Earliest Memories   96
23. Guilt Trips   103
24. Evil Faceless Bureaucrat   106
25. Blood Money   108
26. The Shtetl Market in Toronto   111
27. Other Types of Camps   115
28. Drek from California   119
29. The Society   124
30. Moving up North   126
31. The Favorite Child   130
32. Dad hated Sports   134
33. Retail Circus   137
34. Dad's Philosophy to Life   140

35. Food within a Holocaust Family	143
36. Back to Haliburton	147
37. You never Call	150
38. Struggling to Make Sense of Judaism	154
39. Aging Survivors	157
40. Memory Loss	160
41. Poland's Jewish Revival	164
Afterword	167
Acknowledgments	175
Photos	177
Glossary	187
About the Author	191
Bibliography	193
Amsterdam Publishers Holocaust Library	195

In memory of my mother and father, Shifra and Elija Handler, and those family members that perished in the Holocaust, including my grandparents Temerla and Josek Oksenhendler and Tzipora and Wolf Zloczower, my aunts Jentla Sledzik and Mariem Oksenhendler, my uncle Itzhak Zloczower, Estera Oksenhendler, and my precious sisters Laja and Jenta Oksenhendler.

L'dor v'dor, from generation to generation.

FOREWORD

My father killed himself. It's not something that I tend to openly speak about outside the family. He didn't swallow a bottle of pills or hang himself. He slowly and methodically starved himself until he died.

My father was a controlling and stubborn man. He expected and often demanded how things should be. One of his expectations was that my mother would always be there to serve his needs. He was 12 years older and assumed Mom would outlive him. When her health deteriorated – as she suffered a series of strokes and developed dementia – Dad realized that he would eventually be alone and have to look after himself. That was something he was not prepared to accept. He didn't end his life because he was suffering from a terminal illness. He just decided the road ahead wasn't to his liking.

Aside from the way he died, what I remember about his death was feeling relief, but no sadness. He was a difficult person to live with and now I was free from that burden. Still, it took me quite some time to come to terms with how my father decided to die. Was the suffering he experienced the last three months better than the life he would have had in front of him? I suppose there was only so much change in one's life that could be endured, and he was at the point where he'd had enough. It seemed like a prolonged and painful way to die, but hunger was not something new to him. He had survived over five years in a ghetto, labor camps, and concentration camps on starvation diets. The irony was not lost on me.

We were constantly reminded about the Holocaust. "Finish your dinner. We didn't have food like this in the camps." I learned as an adult that this was a common theme within a home of Holocaust survivors. With a regular diet of wartime stories, oblique references to horrible events, and reminders about the Holocaust, it's not hard to start thinking like a survivor.

We were told the stories – bit by bit. I'm not sure how old I was when I was told about the Holocaust, but I was quite young. I've had nightmares my entire life that can be triggered by stress. In one dream, soldiers are banging on our door late at night to take us away. In another, I am being chased by strangers and looking for somewhere to hide. In the third one, I'm in a large shower room with others and gas begins to come out of the showerheads. People panic and there is screaming.

When the topic of the Holocaust was raised at home, it was never explained at a level appropriate for young children; these stories were distressing. Who wants to hear about parents having experienced horrible abuse? Anytime my father talked about his wartime, he became emotional and often cried, leaving me feeling guilty for raising the subject. So I never bothered to ask questions; it wasn't worth the grief that they created.

Now I have regrets. I knew some details, while I should have gotten the full stories. What were your parents like? What did your mother like to cook? How did you celebrate the holidays? What was your bar mitzvah like? What was it like growing up in small *shtetls* [small Jewish communities in Eastern Europe]? Now it's too late.

Not knowing much about my family's history became both an incentive and disincentive to writing my memoir. I was concerned that I wouldn't be able to find enough information. Early on, I considered abandoning the project, but at a certain point I went from being curious to fully-fledged obsessed. The more I uncovered, the more I wanted to learn.

I was always reluctant to write this memoir, but my wife kept insisting that I should. I'm not a historian. Who am I to be writing a Holocaust-themed book? There are already thousands of books about the Holocaust. Does the world really need another one? What ultimately cemented my resolve was the lawless band of conspirators that attacked Capitol Hill on January 6, 2021. One of the participants was parading around, proudly displaying a shirt that said "Camp Auschwitz." He was glorifying a death camp where numerous family members were murdered. It made my blood boil and I decided my voice was needed after all.

The lockdown during the early part of the pandemic provided me with a lot of time to contemplate my life and who I was. One of the things I was not clear on was my parents' story. I knew where they came from and what they endured, but I was missing much of the details, and they were no longer around to answer any questions. If I couldn't tell their story, then it would be forever lost. With the rise of antisemitism, I realized that their stories took on greater importance – not just for my family, but for all of society.

The first time I wrote down my parents' story it was a 2,000-word blog post. That was the extent of what I could recall. Looking back, it contained gaps and inaccuracies. I asked my sister and brother what they remembered, and gradually recalled more over time. There were buried memories that would suddenly pop into my consciousness. Sometimes it was in the middle of a restless night.

Eventually, I found information in archived documents, recorded interviews, databases, research papers, historical accounts, and memoirs. I searched for books that covered life in Bedzin, the various camps my dad was incarcerated in, the deportation of Romanian Jews, and the Transnistria region of Ukraine.

In 1995, my mother agreed to be interviewed by the Shoah Foundation, established by Steven Spielberg in 1994, one year after completing his Academy Award-winning film *Schindler's List*. I had never watched my mother's video. I didn't think I would learn anything new, or maybe I wasn't ready to learn more. I was wrong. The video helped nail down parts of her story. Unfortunately, the interviewer did not dig deep into her history. I suspect interviewers were instructed not to push their subjects. My dad did not want to be interviewed, so I listened to testimony provided by other family members and friends with similar experiences. My cousin Regina Eisenstein was also interviewed by the Shoah Foundation, and she provided valuable details about the Bedzin Ghetto and Auschwitz.

I searched through records held by Yad Vashem, the memorial and museum in Jerusalem dedicated to the victims of the Holocaust. Included in their collection is an archive containing a database of personal information about those who survived and those who were murdered in the Holocaust. The next step in my research was searching through Jewish genealogy databases, including the Jewish Records Indexing (JRI) Poland and Jewish Genealogy sites to find birth, marriage, and death registrations of my ancestors. I constructed a family tree on the Ancestry website to keep track of family members. My search led me to connect with distant relatives that I was unaware of, including cousins in Los Angeles, Denver, Memphis, Brussels,

Australia and Israel. We shared documents and photographs of family members. The story was growing. I thought I had no additional family other than those my parents were in contact with. Some of these cousins were also children of Holocaust survivors reaching out for family connections while others were predominantly interested in genealogy.

I knew that my dad had been in several concentration camps but was unsure of the number and names. One of the important resources turned out to be the Arolsen Archives, located in Bad Arolsen, Germany. This is the world's most comprehensive archive on the victims and survivors of Nazi persecution with information on about 17.5 million people. Archive records were critical in determining the whereabouts of my family during and after the war. I wrote to the Arolsen Archives and several weeks later, I received several hundred scanned copies of documents that were integral in piecing together timelines and locations.

The documents that I received are a testament to the efficiency and thoroughness of the Nazi regime. The records were largely dated late in the war. Even though the regime was collapsing and in chaos, the Germans were still meticulously keeping records. At first, I didn't understand why there weren't additional documents. Then I realized why these records survived while earlier ones did not: it was because there wasn't enough time to destroy them as the Allied troops overran German-held territory. There was no documentation for family members that were sent directly to the gas chambers. The Germans knew better than to directly connect themselves to that level of genocide. The yellowed documents were both typed and handwritten. Some were difficult to read because the ink had faded considerably or the German cursive script was difficult to make out.

This is not just my family's story, but also my journey, trying to connect all the bits and pieces that I had accumulated. There will always be gaps, but it still is a compelling and gut-wrenching story. In the process, the biggest obstacle turned out to be myself. My resistance to placing myself in this memoir and to releasing my emotional response to these stories was the most difficult part of the process. While searching back through my family history and childhood, I learned as much about myself as I did about my ancestors.

It was not until I undertook the writing of this memoir, that I realized it was time to come out from the shadows. In fact, this could be considered my "coming out party."

FAMILY TREES

Oksenhendler Family

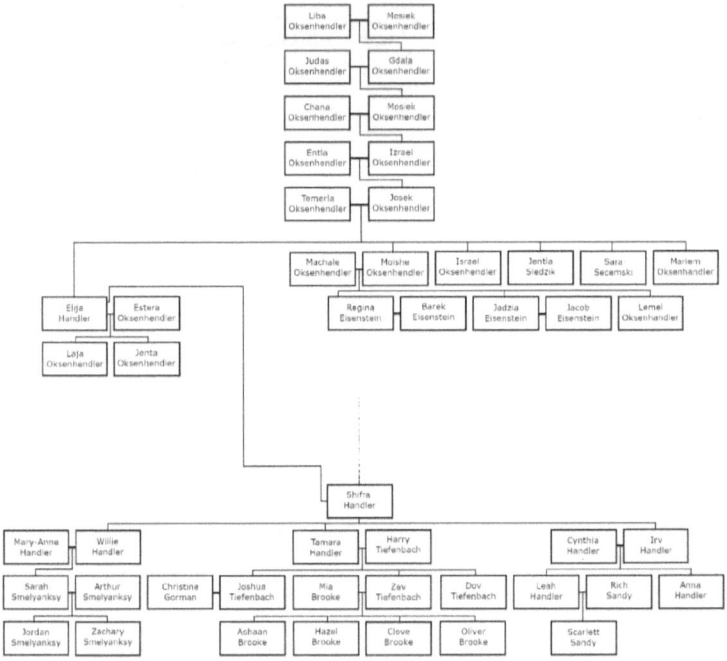

Zloczower Family

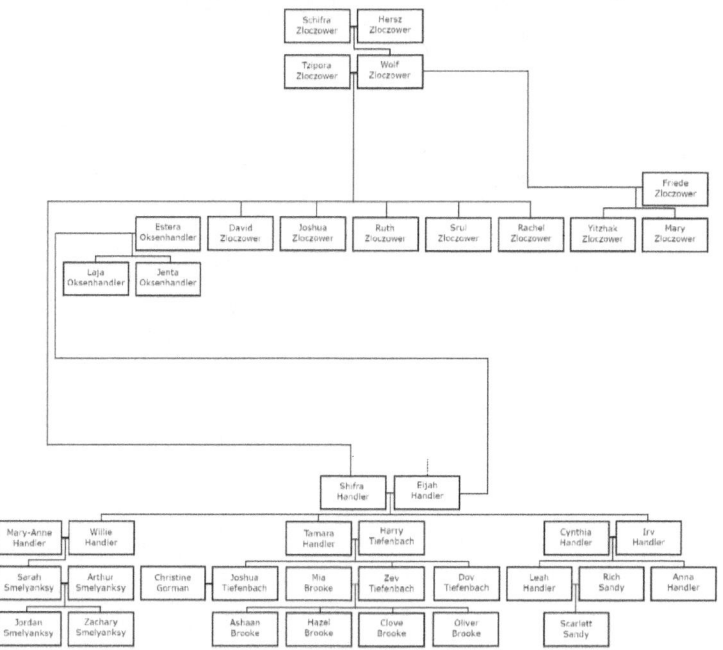

1 PREWAR BEDZIN

My dad, Elija Oksenhendler, was born on November 25, 1912. The surname Oksenhendler is German and translates to cattle or oxen dealer. This provides a clue to my family's background, because in 18th-century Poland, when surnames were first required, these often reflected one's occupation. Family and friends called him Ela, although his Polish legal name was Eliasz. Our surname was shortened to Handler when my family arrived in Canada.

My father's parents, Temerla Tragerman and Josek Oksenhendler, were married in 1899 in Wislica, a village in the Kielce district of south-central Poland. Wislica was considered a shtetl. My grandmother was from a neighboring town, Pinczow, a shtetl with 4,300 Jews, comprising about 60 percent of the population in 1921. My grandparents came from large families.

Following World War I, Wislica had about 1,300 Jewish residents made up of approximately 200 families. The village had a synagogue and two small informal houses of prayer located in homes referred to as *shtiebel* [little house]. Down the street from the synagogue was a Jewish cemetery. Most of the Jews of Wislica were craftsmen or traders like my ancestors who were trading, selling, and butchering livestock. Jewish institutions such as the synagogue, and the Jewish religious school, and salaried jobs such as rabbi and gravedigger were supported by the community through fees charged for kosher slaughtering of meat. This was a common source of community funds since almost all shtetl Jews would only eat kosher meat.

I traced back the Oksenhendler family in Wislica for six generations to my fourth great-grandfather, Mosiek Oksenhendler, born in 1758, and his wife, Liba Federman, born in 1759. Prior to the 18th century, Polish Jews were not legally required to have surnames. You would be identified by your first name and the first names of your parents, for example, Simon, son of Jakub and Roza. This made it impossible to trace back my ancestors beyond the mid-18th century. Leading up to World War I almost every generation of Oksenhendler was born and died in Wislica. Early in the 20th century, some of my grandfather's siblings left Wislica. His brother Symcha moved to Bedzin in 1900, while his brothers David and Zelman, and his sister Dora, emigrated to America seven years later.

Jews and Poles in Wislica coexisted, but relations were not necessarily harmonious. In a 1913 letter written to family members prior to *Rosh Hashanah* [Jewish New Year], my great-grandfather Izrael Gdala Oksenhendler complained about antisemitism in the village. The local priest would stand in front of Jewish businesses and dissuade Poles from shopping there.

Around 1930, my grandparents had enough and moved the family to the much larger Bedzin where the Jewish population in was about 20 times bigger.[1] Jews were drawn to Bedzin, not just because of economic opportunities, but also because it was a Jewish cultural and religious hub. It was referred to as the "Jerusalem of Zaglebie." With its clothing factories and mining operations, Bedzin had employment opportunities that weren't available in small villages.

And my dad's oldest brother, Moishe, married Machela Secemski who was from the nearby village of Działoszyce, a shtetl that was almost 90 percent Jewish prior to the Holocaust. They settled in Działoszyce but followed the rest of the family to Bedzin to escape the poverty in the village.

I knew little about my dad's family because he never spoke of those who didn't survive. He never talked about his parents and their large families. I wasn't even aware that he lived in Wislica for the first 18 years of his life. Genealogy research shows that my grandfather had nine siblings and my grandmother had seven. My dad (born in 1912) had five siblings: Moishe (born in 1901), Jentla (born in 1906), Israel (born in 1910), Sara (born in 1919) and Mariem (born in 1927).

---

1. Bedzin is a town in the Zaglebie Dabrowskie area of Poland, which is a geographical and historical region and currently part of the Upper Silesian province.

In the mid-1930s, Dad opened a butcher business in Bedzin's old Jewish market square where he sold poultry and eggs. As was the case in every Jewish shtetl, a *shochet* [person trained to kill animals according to the Jewish dietary laws] would visit the stall to slaughter the chickens. Everyone in the Jewish community ate kosher food and some Poles would also purchase meat from Jewish merchants. My disabled grandfather had a stand in the back of dad's store where he sold some fruits and vegetables. During a serious fall he had injured both legs. Since he never received medical attention his legs never healed properly. As a result, he walked with the aid of two canes.

Both Dad's brothers, Moishe and Israel, were also butchers, and owned similar businesses because that was the type of merchants the family had always been. All the butchers were in one section of the market, which meant that the brothers competed amongst themselves. They would even bad-mouth their siblings to dissuade customers from buying from the others. There is nothing unusual about sibling rivalry, but in our family, at times, it felt like animosity.

According to a Jewish census conducted in Bedzin in 1939, my dad was living with his parents, along with Mariem when the Germans invaded Poland. That census listed the names, birthdates, addresses, and occupations of 22,167 Jewish residents. It was later used to send able-bodied Jewish residents, including my father and his brothers, to forced labor camps. All but 14 pages survived the war.

My grandparents lived in an apartment at 38 Malachowskiego Street (renamed Kattowitzer Strasse by the Germans) which was the main street in the Jewish quarters. It was a wide, tree-lined boulevard in the town center. Across the street was the Bejt Jakow religious school for girls and a municipal public female Jewish school. My cousins, Regina and Jadzia spent the mornings in the public school and the afternoons in the religious school. Behind my grandparents' apartment at 64 Modrzejowska Street (called Marktstrasse during the war years) was the shtiebel where my family prayed.

The core of the town was 80 percent Jewish with Poles mostly living in the outer perimeter. After getting married in 1940, my father and his young family moved into a smaller apartment at 71 Modrzejowska Street.

Dad received little education as he was pulled out of school at an early age to help support the family. His lack of education was often a liability, but his willingness to take on physical work defined who he was in many respects. At only five feet, three inches, and about 120 pounds he was very proud of his physical strength. Before the war, he was raising a calf for slaughter. The calf had gotten loose in a snowstorm. When he finally found the calf, it was unable or unwilling to walk, so he carried it home on his back. Later, he told me that his strength and endurance were critical to his survival in the *Lager* [camps]. He would remind the guards that he worked harder than any of the Hungarians; hard work was a form of currency.

As proud as he was of his strength, he did not want his children working that hard. We were expected to get a good education and become professionals. I earned two master's degrees and worked as a senior manager with the Ontario government. I don't think he was disappointed by that.

What stands out for me regarding prewar Poland is that there were over 1,400 shtetls, while none exist today. The cultural milieu that defined Polish Jewry was destroyed in less than five years. Prior to World War II, 3.5 million Jews were living in Poland which made up the largest Jewish population in Europe. For centuries, Jews migrated to Poland because of religious tolerance and social autonomy, which ended in the 18th century. Many Polish Jews never assimilated into the general population – unlike German Jews – and continued to live in shtetls.

Jews lived in Bedzin from the end of the Middle Ages. The size of the Jewish population grew rapidly during the industrialization period in the 19th century. Prior to World War II, one of the highest concentrations of Jews existed in Bedzin. The town had a population of about 54,000 and nearly half of the residents (24,000) were Jewish. Although Warsaw had a much larger Jewish population (350,000 prior to World War II), Jews only comprised 30 percent of the city's residents. About two-thirds of the population living in the center of Bedzin were Jewish, while poorer Catholics lived in rundown neighborhoods just outside of the town center. Within a few kilometers, there were two additional towns with significant Jewish populations: Sosnowiec and Dabrowa Gornicza.

Bedzin had a vibrant Orthodox-Jewish community with many social and cultural institutions, not just synagogues and a Jewish cemetery. These included a Jewish hospital, a home for the aged, numerous charitable organizations, a well-recognized orphanage, as well as four Jewish religious schools. The Bedzin Jews supported Yiddish newspapers such as *Zaglembier Tsaytung*, *Dose Jidiszhe Wochenblat*, live theater, and movie houses. My father never went to prayer services at the main synagogue, which was situated at 24 Kołłataja Avenue, but instead to one of the smaller shtiebels that operated in the Jewish quarters. According to Karolina and Piotr Jakowenko, the founders of the Cukerman's Gate Foundation, there were no less than 80 places of worship spread across the city. There was a prayer group to serve every sect in town, each with its own rabbi. The main Bedzin synagogue was used only on Sabbath and holidays. The most observant Jews were *Hassidic* [ultra-observant Jews that originated in Eastern Europe in the 18th century]. My father's family were observant, but not Hassidic. There were two rival religious sects in Bedzin – Mizrachi and Agudah. Mizrachi – sometimes referred to as Zionist Orthodox – Jews followed Jewish laws, including enforcing dietary laws and observance of the Sabbath. They were Zionist and were considered more modern or progressive. Agudah Jews were much more conservative and opposed Zionism.

On Sabbath and Jewish holidays, my father closed his shop as did all Jewish businesses, which meant that much of the town's market was deserted on those days. The streets would then be filled with hundreds of Jews in their black silk topcoats and *shtreimlech* [the fur-edged hats worn by Hassidim], with *gartln* [the rope-like belts worn during prayers] wrapped around their hips, and large prayer books under their arms.

Bedzin Jews were socially, culturally, and economically diverse. They held quite a few seats on the town council. Musicians, Samuel Szpilman and Wladyslaw Szpilman, poets Samuel Cylger and Stanislaw Wygodzki, and painters, Izak Lusze and Roman Baum, spent time in Bedzin. There were Talmudic scholars, craftsmen, merchants, professionals, although more than half of the Jews worked in the trades. At the same time, there were beggars; poverty in the community required the support of philanthropists. One wealthy family provided considerable support to the Jewish orphanage in town.

In general, relations between Jews and Poles were cordial, while the two groups kept their distance. They did business between each other but were socially apart even when living in close proximity. Occasionally, an undercurrent of antisemitism would come to the surface. The region had many ethnic Germans who were referred to as *Volksdeutsch* [people whose language and culture had German origins but were not German citizens], who bought into the antisemitic propaganda coming out of Nazi Germany.

As Jewish persecution in Germany increased, so did the number of organized antisemitic activities. My cousin Regina complained about boycotts of Jewish businesses organized in 1937. Many survivors from Bedzin that I got to know complained about antisemitism. They had stones thrown at them or were beaten, and their property was vandalized.

During the 1920s, the Polish government excluded Jews from receiving government bank credits, public sector employment, and business licenses. During the 1930s, limits were placed on Jewish enrolment in universities, on Jewish shops, and on Jewish admission to the medical and legal professions. While in 1921 and 1922, 25 percent of students were Jews, by 1938 and 1939 – the last school year before the German invasion – the proportion had fallen to a mere eight percent as restrictions on Jewish students were implemented. In the four years prior to the Nazi invasion and occupation, there were numerous anti-Jewish incidents and boycotts of Jewish businesses.

2 PREWAR COMANESTI

My mother, Shifra Zloczower, was born on November 4, 1924, in Comanesti, a tiny village about 20 kilometers from Suceava. Unlike the Polish shtetls where Jews were often half the population, Comanesti was less than 10 percent Jewish. My mother's parents were Wolf and Tzipora. Everyone in the village called my grandfather by his Yiddish name, Velvel (which is also my Yiddish name). Comanesti was situated in the southern Bukovina region which is in northeast Romania at the edge of the Carpathian Mountain and surrounded by lush forests. Today Bukovina is divided between Romania and Ukraine.[1] My mother's photos show that the shtetl was nestled in rolling farmland.

My maternal great-grandfather, Hersz Zloczower, operated a brandy distillery, and his sons went into the business, including my grandfather, Wolf. Hersz was originally from the Galicia region (part of Austria-Hungary – along with his wife Shifra, and three sons – Abraham, Wolf, and Isac – and daughter, Minna. The business mostly catered to the small Jewish community in Comanesti and the surrounding villages. The cherry brandy called *vishnik* was sold in barrels along with homemade wine.

---

1. Bukovina was referred to as the "Switzerland of the East" because of its multi-ethnic character. The ethnic and religious communities coexisted for years without violence. In the 1930s, the situation changed radically, as totalitarian and xenophobic influences from Germany, Italy, and other European states changed attitudes in Romania. In the years between the two World Wars, the Iron Guard became the most successful political movement on the far right, promoting a mixture of nationalism and xenophobia, and pushing Romanian authorities to pursue a policy of harsh antisemitism.

When my grandfather married his first wife, he left the family distillery and opened his own business. He did quite well, and the family lived comfortably until the 1930s when the Great Depression and rising antisemitism significantly impacted his business. The family expertise continued beyond World War II. My mother's cousin, Shmuel Zloczower, emigrated to Israel in 1947 and created the Israeli liqueur Sabra, which is made with oranges and chocolate. He lived next door to orange groves which were his inspiration.

Using the old family recipe, my mom made *vishnik* when I was growing up. I always called it "Jewish moonshine."[2] That stuff had quite a kick, and I remember getting tipsy at a young age. I tell this joke that I had once gone seven years without having a drink until my parents gave me some cherry brandy on my eighth birthday. It was served either straight up or cut down with seltzer water. Before the existence of designer sparkling water, there was seltzer water that was delivered in wooden crates to our front door. The bottle had a cylinder with a lever that released carbon dioxide into the water. Seltzer water was very popular with Eastern European Jews who used it as a digestive aid.

Mom was the youngest of eight children. She had a framed family portrait, which was taken in the late 1920s when she was about four years old. It shows six siblings, including two sisters who were already living in America, whose photos were glued onto the portraits, and if you look closely, you can see that their head are slightly larger. My mother had never mentioned that there was another brother. I didn't know about him until I listened to her Shoah Foundation interview in which she mentioned her oldest brother. I contacted my cousin, Ilan Basch, in New York and asked if he was aware of his name. Ilan wasn't sure who I was referring to but indicated his own middle name, Itzhak, was his grandfather's name. That was the unnamed brother. Itzhak was married with three children and living in Czernowitz by the time my mother was born. I found it strange that the portrait included two siblings in America, but not the one who lived less than 100 kilometers away.

Mom's siblings were Mary (born in 1899), Ruth (1906), Israel (1910), Joshua (1913), David (1916), and Rachel (1918). Tzipora was the mother to all my mother's siblings, except for the two oldest. Itzhak and Mary's

---

2. The brandy recipe was simple: cherries, lots of sugar, and a generous amount of vodka. The mixture was placed in a large jar covered with cheesecloth and rubber bands to allow the gases during fermentation to escape while keeping bugs out. When the fermentation was completed, the jar was stored in the basement. The smell was overpowering.

mother was Wolf's first wife, Friede Renert. She passed away during childbirth in 1902, at the age of 36. The baby also did not survive. Wolf and Friede were married in 1889 and had another child that died after eight days. Families were often large, but child mortality was high.

My grandfather and the rest of the family were observant Orthodox Jews, although not Hassidic. Over the eight days of Passover observance, they would not only eat *matzah* [unleavened bread], but would also replace much of their food, dishes, and cooking utensils for the eight days. My grandmother would bake her own matzah for the holiday, and the home would be meticulously cleaned to remove *chametz* [food such as bread and other grains].

When I was a child, my mother would continue this holiday ritual even while working full-time in the family business. My grandfather would fill barrels of water from their well and not draw water directly from the well during Passover. Mom said that the barrel water would develop an unpleasant taste and odor by the end of the holiday. She had no explanation for this practice. It might be a ritual related to the story of Passover where Moses was pulled from the river. A more likely reason was the concern that chametz might contaminate the well, making the well water prohibited over the holiday.

According to my mother relations between the Jews and Gentiles in Comanesti were mostly good, but the situation deteriorated during the 1930s. Antisemitism increased in Romania, and my mother was expelled from school in 1936. Her father hired a tutor to maintain her Hebrew studies, but in the end she received little education.

My mother lived in a tiny close-knit community surrounded by a large supportive family. I was surprised to learn that her small village of Comanesti with about 20 Jewish families had two synagogues. One was used by the Hassidic Jews, while the non-Hassidic Jews prayed at the *Alte Shul* [Old Synagogue], which was across the street from my mother's house. The *shul* [synagogue] was managed by my grandfather who served as its *shamas* [the person responsible for its day-to-day functioning]. It was more of a shtiebel and far less formal than a synagogue. My mother was assigned the task of waxing and polishing the floor each week before the Sabbath. Women didn't participate in services but would listen to the men chanting the prayers from outside the building. The members led their own services but on holidays and High Holy Days, they brought in prayer leaders from Suceava, the neighboring town. On the holidays, Jews came from nearby villages to pray at the synagogues. I came across a story where right before

Rosh Hashanah members of my grandfather's synagogue "borrowed" the Torah scroll from the Hassidic synagogue; the Hassidim were not very pleased that they had to pray with the non-Hassidim on the High Holy Days.

Despite its small size, Comanesti's Jewish community lacked a Jewish cemetery, so burials were done in Suceava. There was a *mikvah* [ritual bath], in which observant married Jewish women were required to immerse themselves once a month after their menstrual cycle. It was only used during the winter months; at other times the village fishponds were used. The village also had a shochet, who ensured that there was kosher meat available for the Jewish residents. Abraham Dawid Schachter, the rabbi at the Hassidic synagogue was also a *mohel*, a person performing *brises* [religious circumcisions] for people in the village and the surrounding area. After my grandfather's sister, Minna, married in 1902, she moved to Parhoutz, about 10 kilometers away, and when she had a baby two years later, my great-grandfather arranged for Rabbi Schachter to conduct the bris.

At the start of World War II, Romania sided with Nazi Germany. It succeeded in holding off an attack in 1940 by allowing Nazi Germany to carve up Romania, ceding northern Transylvania back to Hungary; northern Bukovina and Bessarabia to the Soviet Union; and Dobruja to Bulgaria. Romania had lost about 30 percent of its territory and, in effect, had become a satellite of Germany. Although the northern section of Bukovina fell under the control of Russia, Comanesti and Suceava in the south remained under Romanian administration. When the Romanian army retreated from previously held regions, its soldiers attacked and killed Jewish civilians. As usual, Jews were the scapegoats, and were labeled as communist sympathizers. As was the case in Poland and other European countries, rising antisemitism in the 1930s was accepted as part of the usual cycle of hate directed at Jews and would subside over time.

One Friday evening in 1938, my mother heard voices outside their home. It was late in the evening, and she was the only person awake in the household. Flames appeared at the window and when she looked out she saw gentile villagers setting fire to their house. She leaped to her feet, shouting everyone awake, and they fled the house. The arsonists wouldn't allow them to extinguish the flames, but my grandfather got hold of the local priest with whom he had a good relationship. The priest convinced the villagers to put out the fire. There was only minimal damage to the exterior of the house, but the incident traumatized the family. Since the attack, my mother always insisted on sleeping with the blinds or shades open.

3 BEDZIN GHETTO

Normal life ended for Polish Jews when Germany invaded Poland on September 1, 1939. In response, refugees came streaming through the streets of Bedzin: farmers with cows and wagons, some on foot with buggies, packages, and bags – soon followed by German tanks and armored vehicles. The German Tenth Army invaded from the south, entering Bedzin and the neighboring towns of Sosnowiec and Dabrowa Gornicza on September 4. The Polish army offered no resistance.

The war did not come as a surprise. Hitler had not hidden his intentions. He considered Poland to be an illegitimate state that was created following the end of World War I. Similarly Vladimir Putin considered Ukraine to be an illegitimate state before invading in 2022. Hitler withdrew from a non-aggression pact with Poland early in 1939 and negotiated a similar pact with the Soviet Union just a week before the invasion. Much of Europe had been on edge ever since Nazi Germany had annexed Austria a year earlier, and troop movements in August had signalled an impending invasion. My cousin Regina remembers that her school held drills in the event there was an attack while the school was open.

Even before the Germans invaded Bedzin, word circulated that the Nazis were rounding up and deporting Jewish men. Groups of men left on large commercial wagons drawn by horses to evade the German troops, leaving their families behind. Dad and his brother Israel were part of this exodus, heading to the East and crossing into Russian-held territory. They would soon return to Bedzin after they realized that they were in as much danger under the Russians.

The persecution of the Jewish population began immediately. The Orthodox were subject to the worst abuses and indignities. They were stopped in the streets, where their beards were forcibly shaved or ripped out, and they were compelled to perform humiliating acts in public.

Within the first few days of the occupation, Jewish properties were seized, and shops were closed. All Jews, including my father, lost their businesses which had a devastating impact on the community. The rationale often provided was that the Jews invited such action for raising the prices of food or hiding goods. Mobile death squads appeared in the first week and about 100 Bedzin residents were shot, including several prominent members of the Jewish community. Jews were only permitted to travel on certain streets and could no longer enter public facilities. Food rationing was introduced. A curfew was imposed, and Jews were required to wear a white armband with a Star of David.

On the evening of September 8, the Germans organized a pogrom – a Russian word in origin, meaning "to wreak havoc" – during which the main synagogues in Bedzin, Sosnowiec, and Dabrowa Gornicza were attacked and destroyed with a crowd of worshippers inside for Sabbath services. This was a typical practice of the Nazis – destroy the local synagogues to inflict terror and pain on the Jewish community.

My uncle Moishe's family fled Bedzin at the start of the war to his wife's ancestral home in Dzialoszyce. They believed that it would be safer in a smaller community. Prior to the war, Dzialoszyce had lost many of their youth and younger families because of a lack of economic opportunities. Hundreds returned as the war broke out, often by foot, hoping it might be safer there. It created a refugee crisis since the community was unable to support all those who suddenly appeared.

My uncle and his family did not stay long there. When they returned, my cousin Regina learned about the Bedzin synagogue attack from a close friend who lived in an apartment next to the synagogue. Her friend described the scene that night. German soldiers broke down the entrance gates of the houses adjacent to the synagogue, threw in incendiary bombs, and ordered everyone out, claiming that Jews fired at them from within the synagogue. The Nazi soldiers – assisted by some locals – used incendiary bombs on multiple buildings, including the synagogue building and the nearby *Bet Midrash* [Jewish study hall dedicated to Torah study]. The flames rapidly spread to five neighboring apartment buildings inhabited by Jews. The family of Regina's friend managed to escape. Not everyone was so fortunate. People tried to escape the burning buildings, some jumping out of windows while carrying Torah scrolls. They were systematically shot by the Germans, and their bodies thrown in the flames. Some people managed to escape and jumped into the nearby river to extinguish their burning clothes. About 60 were killed. The victims were buried in a mass grave in the Czeladz cemetery; most of the bodies were so burnt that they couldn't be identified. The day after the attack the streets were littered with bodies.

A group of 50 Jews fled to the Holy Trinity church, which was up the hill adjacent to the synagogue. While fleeing, German soldiers fired at them, wounding a few. When the remaining Jews reached the church gates, Mieczysław Zawadzki, the church's young parish priest, brought everyone in and instructed the nuns to treat the wounds and offer first aid. Once they were treated, he asked the Jews to leave under the cover of darkness through the back gate where things were safer. For his actions, in 2007, Father Mieczysław Zawadzki was posthumously declared Righteous Among the Nations by Yad Vashem.

A ghetto was formed in the center of Bedzin. This was not a walled-in ghetto like those in most Polish cities and towns. Certain streets were off limits to Jews and made available to Germans who resettled in Bedzin. Jews living on these streets were removed from their apartments and were forced to live with Jewish families in Jewish-designated streets. Our family was more fortunate than many, at least for a time. They lived on Malachowskiego and Modrzejowska Streets within the Jewish quarters and were allowed to remain in their apartments.

In October 1939, the Germans deported 10,000 Jews from neighboring communities of the Zagłebie Dabrowskie region into Bedzin, where they joined the 24,000 Jews already present. In April 1941, Jews from Oswiecim (Auschwitz) were also forced to resettle in Bedzin (or neighboring Sosnowiec), since their homes were taken over by families of the SS guards that were assigned to the expanding Auschwitz-Birkenau concentration camp complex. It took several months to disperse them to private apartments which now had to accommodate multiple families.

The Germans required that the Jews of Bedzin and Sosnowiec – as well as every other city and town – to form a *Judenrat* [Jewish Council], that was used to assign work, distribute food rations and reassign housing. The Judenrat had to collaborate with their own oppressors, but in the case of the

Bedzin Judenrat, they willingly cooperated. Because Dad was unskilled, he was assigned menial work, which mostly consisted of cleaning public toilets and streets, or working as a porter. Those with skills deemed valuable to the Germans were assigned factory work, in particular at the clothing factories that were converted to manufacture military uniforms.

The Judenrat would eventually designate my father as dispensable and had him deported to forced labor camps where he had to fight to survive. I get no satisfaction knowing that the Judenrat members were even less fortunate than he was. They thought they might save themselves by cooperating with the Nazis. It didn't work out that way. They were sent to the Auschwitz gas chambers just a little over a year later when they were also deemed dispensable by the Germans. It is ironic that some people who were sent to labor camps, such as my father, managed to survive while all the Judenrat members were murdered.

Poles were not exempt from persecution. Silesia contained a considerable number of ethnic Germans who resented being part of Poland. Unlike the rest of Poland, which was considered occupied territory, Silesia was annexed by the Reich and seen as a permanent part of Germany. It was an industrial base that would benefit the German war effort. As a result, Poles fell under certain pressures as an intense program of Germanization was introduced. Polish schools were banned, and in some regions Polish peasants were replaced by German colonists. Bedzin was renamed Bendsburg, and a young bureaucrat named Udo Klausa was sent by Berlin to be its civilian administrator. German became the official language for the region. When I retrieved archival documents regarding my family during my visit in the summer of 2022, the documents from this period were in German.

As strange as it might seem, during this horrible period, people continued to get married and have families. My guess is that people believed things would get better. Centuries of antisemitism in Europe may have created a sense that this was just another cycle of Jew hate and would eventually pass. Conditions in Bedzin weren't as harsh as in other parts of Poland. The factories in the area offered more employment than most Polish ghettos, which sometimes came with slightly better food rations. Ghetto residents were freer to move about and had more opportunities to smuggle in food. So people tried to adapt to the new "normal."

4 FORCED LABOR CAMPS

From November 1940 Jews in Bedzin were sent to forced labor camps. All men between the ages of 17 and 50, and women from 16 to 45, who were not working in a local workshop or factory – in other words, not already supporting the German war machine – could receive a summons from the Judenrat, requiring them to appear before a medical commission. This was yet another selection for workers to be sent to do forced labor. The authorities threatened to "evacuate" all family members of those that failed to report. The likely destination was Auschwitz.

The Nazis operated hundreds of camps that stretched across German-occupied Europe. The forced laborers worked for a broad range of war-related industries, from manufacturing armaments and electronics to sewing army uniforms and other garments. The larger concentration camps had subcamps which were built near factories. The SS would have the prisoners build the subcamps, and then they would rent out the prisoners to private companies, such as Krupp, IG Farben, or Siemens. Forced labor was adopted by the Germans to exploit enemies of the state and to compensate for labor shortages caused by recruitment to the German army. It was no longer a priority once the Nazis adopted genocide as state policy.

Between November 1940 and May 1942, under the direction of the German authorities, about 4,000 Jews were deported from Bedzin to forced labor camps using lists created by the local Judenrat. That was the case for my dad and his two brothers. Dad and Uncle Israel were sent to a camp in Ottmuth in southwest Poland. My uncle Moishe was sent to Greiditz, a subcamp of Auschwitz. My aunt Sara was sent to Bernsdorf, a textile forced labor camp for women and a subcamp of Gross-Rosen. In some cases, the Jewish police, working with the Judenrat, would pick up men on the street or from their homes late at night and send them to forced labor camps.

Many people tried to avoid deportation to the labor camp, preferring to sit out the war in the Bedzin Ghetto. If you were employed in a local factory contributing to the war effort, the Judenrat would not put you on one of the deportation lists. Wealthier Jews who had been able to hide valuables were able to bribe their way off deportation lists. However, in my family's case, the labor camps turned out to provide the best chance of survival; my dad and three of his five siblings survived. No one could have known that the next phase of the persecution of Jews would involve extermination. Family members that remained in Bedzin would eventually be deported to Auschwitz-Birkenau and most were sent directly to the gas chambers.

When Dad and Uncle Israel arrived at Ottmuth, many of the prisoners were forced to construct highways and railway tracks to support the German war effort. Dad and Israel were fortunate to be sent to a local Bata shoe factory to produce army boots.[1]

Those assigned strenuous and hazardous work, such as road and rail construction, did not survive long. The labor camps weren't that much different from concentration camps. Initially, they had no electrified wire fences, no selections, no mass killings, and no uniforms. Prisoners wore the clothes they came with but were required to stitch a Star of David on their jackets. The camps were mostly administered by retired German military personnel. It wasn't until later that the SS or *Schutzstaffel* – the "Protective Squad," which began as a special guard for Adolf Hitler – took over operating the camps.

At Ottmuth Dad slept on a straw spread on the floor. In the mornings he received a piece of stale bread, some margarine and imitation coffee. At 6 a.m., there was an *Appell* [roll call] during which the prisoners were counted, and afterward they were marched off to work. They returned at 6 p.m. for another Appell. These roll calls were standard procedure as every prisoner had to be accounted for. Afterward, they were served a watery soup. There were fixed rations in all the camps; those were meager because the Germans had no interest in sustaining their slave workforce. Guards

---

1. Robert Clary, who is best known for his role in the 1960s TV series Hogan's Heroes, was the most prominent prisoner at Ottmuth and he worked in the same shoe factory. Clary was deported to the camp in 1942 well after my father had left.

were brutal and frequently used whips and vicious dogs; my father was often beaten for no apparent reason.

My father said that some people saved their bread only to have it stolen at night. Therefore he always wolfed down his food rations. He wore the same rags every day and worked in wet clothes if it rained. Although there were no gas chambers, life in these camps was harsh. The Germans didn't need gas chambers to murder their victims.

At some point my father was sent back to Bedzin. In the early years of the war, people were occasionally permitted to return home. I know he was in Bedzin in December 1941 because I was able to retrieve marriage and birth documents from the Bedzin archives that he signed? I imagine that the opportunity to return home provided hope. He might have believed they could survive, and things would work out. In fact, it was the last time he was ever to see Bedzin or his family.

In April 1942, Dad was sent to a labor camp at Rattwitz, also in the southwest region of Poland. I.G. Farben was building a synthetic rubber plant nearby and my father worked on the construction of the factory, carrying bricks and cement blocks to the site. Being transported from one camp to another introduced additional peril. The journeys to the camps were always by train, usually taking several days, and in some cases even weeks. Prisoners were so tightly packed into the freight cars, that it was impossible to sit or kneel. Conditions inside the transports were inhumane, and, for some, lethal. Some prisoners died en route from dehydration, starvation, or suffocation.

Dad wasn't provided with any food or water while being transported. Toilet facilities consisted of a bucket which quickly overfilled. The smell of vomit, urine, and excrement was overpowering, and most transports had no windows or ventilation.

5 THE KAMIONKA GHETTO

My father lived in the Bedzin Ghetto for parts of the first 20 months of Nazi occupation. My cousin Regina, who was in the ghetto until it was liquidated in August 1943, tells in her Shoah interview how the ghettoization process in Bedzin occurred in three stages.

The first stage occurred immediately following the German invasion. Jewish properties and businesses were handed over to a German Trustee. Not only was property confiscated but also cash, jewelry, furs, and other valuables. Confiscated items included books and radios. The Bedzin resistance hid thousands of books in the basement of the orphanage. Any Jew in possession of prohibited articles could be shot.

The second stage occurred several months later with the formal establishment of a ghetto. The ghettos in Upper Silesia differed from the "closed districts" of the General Government, including Warsaw, Krakow, Lublin, and Lviv. The "open" ghetto made it possible for the inhabitants to smuggle in food and other necessities. To accommodate this stage, in early 1940, the Judenrat established a resettlement bureau in the town hall to expel Jews from certain streets. Over time, the area in which Jews were allowed to reside or circulate would shrink, creating overcrowded conditions. Ghettoization was intended to create Jewish-free regions for German settlers. It was considered offensive to interact with a Jew.

The ghetto remained open until 1942 without any physical barriers, because there were businesses and factories within the ghetto boundaries that non-Jews needed to access. Regina worked in a shop on Modrzejowska

Street, which employed 700 to 800 Jews and produced uniforms for the German army. Although food supplies were limited, the Jews in the ghetto did not starve. They had jobs, there was basic medical care available, and there were few beggars in the streets. The ghetto boundaries were enforced by Jewish police and the SS. Jews caught outside after curfew, without their identity cards – or outside the ghetto boundaries – were subject to automatic arrest, imprisonment, or deportation. In some cases, they were shot on the spot.

Public hangings were another tool for maintaining compliance. There was one that took place in April 1941, just down the street where my dad lived. Another took place in April 1942. In her Shoah interview, Regina tells how thousands of factory workers were released from work early and required to witness the hangings of two men who were accused of dealing in the black market. One of the two men had tutored Regina and her sister Jadzia. The hanging was carefully planned out. Worker identity cards were confiscated at factories and shops, and only returned when the worker showed up for the public execution. There was a special viewing area for Germans so that they would be separated from Jews and Poles. Taking photos was forbidden, although someone took the risk of photographing the hanging from a distance.

A good description of life in the ghetto comes from Rutka Laskier, who is considered the Polish Anne Frank.[1] Over time, the ghetto boundaries continued to shrink, making living conditions even worse. Jews selected for forced labor had to report to the local transit camp, known as the Dulag. In Bedzin, it was situated in the former Jewish orphanage, which was conveniently located across from the railway station. Failure to comply resulted in arrest and the withdrawal of the family's ration cards. Transports to labor camps began in 1940, but were expanded in the spring of 1941, after Himmler decided to use Jewish forced labor to construct large factories to support German war production. It was during this period that my dad was sent to Ottmuth forced labor camp. Deportations to death camps didn't occur in large numbers until 1942.

Moniek Merin, who was responsible for the Judenrat in Bedzin and the

---

1. During the first three months of 1943, at the age of 13, she began a diary chronicling her life in the Bedzin Ghetto. She died in Auschwitz later that year. Laskier came to realize she would not survive; and, grasping the importance of her diary as a document of what had happened to the Jewish population of Bedzin, she asked a Polish friend, Stanislawa Sapinska, to hide the diary. After the ghetto was evacuated, Sapinska retrieved the diary and kept it in her home library for 63 years until a family member revealed the existence of the document. The diary was published in 2006.

surrounding towns, was a highly contentious figure. Many Jews believed he was overzealous in carrying out orders from the Germans. In the first days of the occupation, separate Jewish Councils were appointed in Bedzin and Sosnowiec, but early in 1940 the Bedzin council was made subordinate to the *Zentrale der Jüdischen Ältestenräte* [Central Office of the Jewish Councils of Elders] in Upper Silesia, established in Sosnowiec and headed by the increasingly autocratic Moniek Merin. He had no previous leadership role in the Jewish community and appears to have voluntarily offered his services to the Germans. Merin denounced the underground, believing that armed resistance would doom the entire ghetto. Despite his full cooperation with the Nazis, Merin and his fellow council members were arrested and sent to the gas chambers at Auschwitz-Birkenau in June 1943.

Nazi policy called for the exploitation of Jewish labor until it was replaced by its extermination policy. The Zaglebie region had a high concentration of Jewish-owned textile manufacturers that were confiscated by the Nazis and operated by German trustees. The shops or factories were accountable to the Schmelt Organization, established by Reichsführer Heinrich Himmler. Those who worked in one of these shops were considered vital to the war effort and were avoided being sent to one of the Schmelt Organization's forced labor camps. They also earned a meager wage, which provided an opportunity to buy food when it was available. The Schmelt Organization was popular with German industrialists who, later in the war, tried to pressure Himmler to reverse the policy to exterminate the Jews so they could continue to exploit cheap Jewish labor.

One of the largest employers in the region was Alfred Rossner, who arrived in Bedzin in 1940 and took over operating several factories. Rossner worked directly under the SS, producing uniforms for the German armed forces. At one point he employed 6,000 Jews. Production was considered essential to the German war effort, and the Jews who worked for Rossner were provided with a special pass that protected them from deportation. The blue Rossner special pass became a much-coveted possession. Each worker with such a pass was allowed to protect several family members. Thus, single people could protect their parents, and married workers could protect their spouse and up to one child. My cousins, Regina and Jadzia, who worked in Rossner shops had such a pass. My aunt Machela had sold some of their possessions on the black market and used the money to ensure the girls would have a job in a local factory and not be deported to a forced labor camp. The passes protected the rest of the family. They could remain in Bedzin until the final liquidation in August 1943.

Rossner was unlike most German trustees and treated his Jewish workers well, often going out of his way to protect them and their families. He would give them prior warnings of impending deportations and send his German staff to free them at the last moment from the deportation trains. Rossner has been referred to as the Oskar Schindler of Bedzin. According to survivors, during the first large deportation from Bedzin in May 1942, Rossner drove his buggy into the Jewish ghetto shouting in Yiddish to the inhabitants not to be fooled by the summons of the Judenrat and urging them not to report for deportation. In December 1943, after the final deportation from the ghetto, he was arrested by the Gestapo, and was hanged one month later. The exact course of the proceedings and the nature of the charges that were brought against him were not clear, but there is little doubt that his "crime" was related to the help he gave to Jews. On September 28, 1995, Yad Vashem decided to recognize Alfred Rossner posthumously as Righteous Among the Nations.

By late 1942, Bedzin and the nearby Sosnowiec bordering Bedzin became the only cities in the region where Jews could live. It wasn't until January 1943 that the third stage of the Bedzin Ghetto began. The area chosen to house the remaining Jewish population was Kamionka, a rural and rundown neighborhood between Bedzin and Dabrowa Gornicza. After the deportation that took place in August 1942, the local German administrators realized that they would not get the Jewish population to voluntarily show up for deportation or be able to trick them into showing up to check identity cards. What they devised was to cordon off the remaining Jews into a small area where they could be forcibly removed without means to escape.

Kamionka had been inhabited by the most impoverished Poles, living in substandard housing without running water or toilets. Each tiny house – which had, at one time, accommodated a single Polish family – would house up to three Jewish families. Some families were forced to live in makeshift tents by stretching sheets on poles or furniture. Conditions with respect to food, drinking water, and sanitation bordered on disastrous.

When I visited Poland in August 2022, I walked the streets of Kamionka and found it unsettling. The area had been rebuilt but the streets were still narrow with small spartan houses. You could visualize what it would have been like in 1943.

Each week Jews living outside this designated area had to move out of their homes and were assigned a place to live in the Kamionka Ghetto by the Judenrat. People took with them as many of their possessions as they could.

Each day there would be a steady procession of people moving into the ghetto. If some furnishing wouldn't fit in the space assigned, items were left outside. This process took several months to complete. At this point, Machela had six children to look after. Her brother, Simcha Secemski, had been conscripted by the Polish army prior to fight the German invasion in 1939. He was killed in the early days of the war. His wife was eventually deported to one of the camps and Machela took in their three children. The seven of them were ordered to move into the Kamionka Ghetto, living in one tiny decrepit house.

6 EXTERMINATION THROUGH WORK

It was German industrialist Alfred Krupp who recommended to Adolph Hitler that Jews be exploited as slave labor. At the time he was one of the largest armament manufacturers in the world. Krupp recognized the financial advantages of slave labor and supported the concept of "extermination through work." For years, my dad and other survivors boycotted German goods. When I purchased my first car, an Audi, after completing graduate school, my father was not pleased. As it turned out, the car had bad karma and was constantly in the shop.

The SS had established the Economic and Administration Organization to review applications from businesses that wished to use forced labor workers and prisoners of war. Once approved, a subcamp would be constructed close to the factory. This is the reason why many concentration camps had so many subcamps. The subcamps were built by the prisoners next to a factory. The cost of construction and supplies, such as beds and barbed wire, would be covered by the factory owners. The SS was responsible for guarding the prisoners and their clothing and food. Prisoners would be leased to the factories from the SS for a daily fee of four or six Reichsmarks depending on their skills.

Two months into my dad's time in Rattwitz, IG Farben decided to abandon the construction of the plant at this location. Dad was transferred to Markstädt, a subcamp of Gross-Rosen and one of the larger forced labor camps in Germany with 3,000 prisoners. My father would remain within the Gross-Rosen camp system until the last two months of the war.

Markstädt was located just outside Breslau, Germany – now Wroclaw, Poland – and next to several factories where war materials were manufactured. He was assigned a job working for the Krupp conglomerate.

Some of the camps that my father was sent to had at their entrance the infamous sign *Arbeit macht Frei* [Work sets you free]. The work was intended to kill you. My dad insisted that the work kept him alive. That's not to say that he was accepting of the situation. He never got over his bitterness, and the reparation payments (800 Deutschmarks per month by the time he was in his nineties) he received after the war never properly compensated him for what he endured or what he lost.

Even calling the Jewish workforce slave labor is a misnomer. Slave owners traditionally saw value in slave ownership and kept their human assets alive. The Jewish workers were considered less than slaves. Krupp and the industrialists also used captured foreign civilians and prisoners of war as forced labor. They were also treated harshly but more likely to survive.

At Markstädt Dad worked at a Krupp artillery factory, manufacturing gun parts. Twice a week, he had a strip shorn from his forehead to the nape of his head. No explanation was provided, and I suspect it was just another form of humiliation that prisoners had to endure. The guards at Markstädt were brutal and hundreds of prisoners died from beatings. Dad was frequently beaten, and at one point all his teeth were knocked out. What did he do to deserve these beatings? He was Jewish.

On November 25, 1943, an unusual selection took place. Three thousand Jews were kept naked in the snow for hours until they were ordered to run several hundred meters to the barracks, where an SS officer and doctor sat on chairs, sentencing hundreds of weak and emaciated Jews to be gassed. Dad survived the selection. It was his 31st birthday. The next day he and a large group of the survivors from the selection were marched six kilometers to the Fünfteichen camp (also a Gross-Rosen subcamp), which had just been completed. The camp was established to provide a workforce for a newly built Krupp armaments plant. Dad was put to work producing 75mm and 150mm cannons.

His workday at Fünfteichen was 12 hours long, seven days a week. Each day began at 5 a.m. when the prisoners got up and cleaned the barracks. He received no breakfast, only hot watered-down tea that he had to line up for. At the start and end of the working day an Appell was conducted that typically took an hour or more. In the morning, corpses were removed from the barracks of those that died overnight and included in the count with the living. After the morning roll call, Dad was marched three kilometers to the Krupp factory on a dirt road lined with barbed-wire fencing on both sides to prevent escapes. The SS, walking outside the fencing, escorted the prisoners with dogs.

Each barracks was administered by a *Kapo,* a prisoner assigned by the Nazis to supervise their peers. Dad witnessed many fellow prisoners dying from mistreatment. About 100 prisoners died each week. Beatings were common and typically inflicted by Kapos, but SS guards often joined in. The beatings took place not just at the camp but in the factory. One could be beaten for leaving a workstation without permission, talking to another prisoner, or even sitting down for a moment to rest. Beatings could be fatal. Each day there were suicides by prisoner who could not tolerate the conditions. You need to be both physically and mentally tough to survive.

Factory work provided opportunities to escape. Because shifts were 12 hours long, escapes often occurred on the night shift or in the evening, when the day shift prisoners were finishing work. Dad never considered escaping because there was nowhere to go. He felt the civilian population in Germany would turn him in. Prisoners shot while attempting to escape were hung and put on display in the assembly area as a warning to others. There might have been a sign on the prisoner's chest stating, *Ich bin von Reise zurück* [I am back from my trip]. If an escaped prisoner was captured alive, he would be brought to the assembly area to be hanged in front of the other prisoners.

The morning ration consisted of 200 grams of stale bread and a small square of margarine. After the evening roll call, the prisoners were fed. Dad explained dinner was usually just a single bowl of thin soup, which was mostly water. He told me that the only contents of the soups were stones. This was not a total exaggeration, as they often put spinach into the soup, which typically hadn't been washed, and was therefore full of dirt and stones. Cabbage or turnips that were only suitable for livestock were sometimes thrown into the soup pot. Those in the front of the line for soup received mostly water; the few vegetables that were thrown in were at the bottom. In some cases, those who were ladling out the soup were bribed so that they would reach deeper into the pot for some vegetables. Dad was a hard worker, and he was able to parlay that into an occasional extra ration of bread or an easier work assignment from a sympathetic camp guard. To be blunt, my father became well versed in the art of larceny, lying, and ass-licking.

After the Germans attacked Russia, Russian prisoners of war were sent to the camps. Harry Ferens, a friend of my father from Bedzin was also in Fünfteichen. In his Shoah Foundation interview Harry stated that he witnessed Russian prisoners removing the liver of a dead comrade and eating it. I doubt this was an isolated occurrence. Prisoners were starving and desperate leading to the breakdown of taboos.

Every aspect of prisoner life was brutal. The barracks my father was assigned to had two long rooms for sleeping and a common room. There were about 100 men in each room in leaky, uninsulated wooden barracks. They slept on wooden bunk beds that were sometimes layered with straw bedding. The bunks were theoretically designed to hold three people per tier, but they typically slept six or more. A top bunk was prized by the inmates because the straw bedding was fouled by sick prisoners and would leak down to those sleeping in lower bunks. The barracks lacked sanitation and were infested with rats, lice, and other vermin. Dad was fortunate that he never contracted typhus, which was always present. It was almost impossible to avoid catching lice in these crowded conditions, where people lived on top of each other. They would spring from one person to the next. During selections, the SS would look for scratch marks on prisoners, an indication that they had lice, and these people were often among the first to be removed. The Germans created conditions where lice proliferated, and then killed anyone that had them.

The Nazis often selected people with criminal backgrounds to be Kapos. Dad said there were some sympathetic Kapos, but most were as bad as the SS. Kapos minimized costs by allowing camps to function with fewer SS personnel. The system was designed to turn victim against victim, as the Kapos treated their fellow prisoners harshly to maintain the favor of their SS overseers. If they were derelict, they would be returned to the status of ordinary prisoners.

7 EXPULSION FROM COMANESTI

Mom wasn't quite 16 when the hostilities spread to Romania. The villagers learned of the Nazi atrocities firsthand from Jews fleeing Nazi-occupied Poland. The Polish Jews would pass through their village, trying to find passage to Palestine. In the summer of 1940, the Romanian army withdrew from northern Bucovina and Bessarabia, after being attacked by the Soviet army. Suddenly, Jews were considered communists and became associated with the enemy. The retreating soldiers and local gendarme triggered pogroms in villages and towns throughout the region to cleanse the area of Jews.

On Friday evening August 2, 1940, as the Sabbath was beginning, the pogroms reached Comanesti. Romanian soldiers and civilians destroyed all Jewish homes and attacked its residents. This was two years after local fascists tried to burn down my mother's house. Fortunately, my mother and her family fled from their home and managed to hide in a nearby field. The home and all their possessions were destroyed. All that remained was rubble.

During the attack, the Comanesti Rabbi, Lieb Schachter, and his two sons were tortured and killed, and their bodies dumped at the edge of the village. The rabbi's wife was shot while lighting the Sabbath candles at home. Three other Jews were killed in the Comanesti pogrom until the Jews of Suceava were able to get the authorities to intervene on the following evening. The pogrom was stopped, but that was the end of the Jewish community in Comanesti.

The Jews in the villages were now homeless. They were ordered to move to Suceava where Jewish citizens were expected to house them. The same scenario occurred in the surrounding villages. About 2,000 Jews from the region were deported to Suceava, which was already home to almost 4,000 Jews. With two siblings in New York, one in Palestine, one married and living elsewhere, and one in the Romanian army, there were five remaining family members who relocated to Suceava: my mother, her parents, and her siblings Rachel and David. They knocked on doors of Jewish residents, looking for a sympathetic family who would board them. They found a family willing to take them in, but there was no room for my mother. My grandfather found a wealthy Jewish family that accepted her. However, they did not take her in out of charity. They had lost their domestic servant and had my mother work in her place. Mom was mistreated by the owners, which is especially heartbreaking because they were also Jewish.

In September 1940, the Romanian monarch was forced to abdicate, and a coalition government was formed under Marshall Ion Antonescu and the antisemitic Iron Guard. It consisted of radical right-wing military officers. Shortly afterwards, Romania signed the Tripartite Pact and entered World War II on the Axis side. The new Romanian coalition quickly announced several restrictive measures against the Jews, which mirrored the Nazi's racial laws. In addition, Iron Guard thugs arbitrarily robbed or seized Jewish-owned businesses and assaulted and sometimes killed Jewish citizens in the streets. There were numerous pogroms during this period, and these were part of the arrangement between Hitler and Antonescu.

In June 1941, Operation Barbarossa – the Axis invasion of the Soviet Union – took place. German and Romanian troops took back northern Bukovina and Bessarabia and immediately murdered Jews in those regions. The murder of Jews spread into southern Bukovina in July 1941. Special action squads called *Einsatzgruppen,* made up of Nazi SS units and police, moved on the heels of the advancing German army. Their job was to kill any Jews they could find in the occupied territory.

In Suceava life became difficult. As was the case in other Nazi-occupied communities, there was a 6 p.m. to 8 a.m. curfew for Jews and a requirement that they wear a yellow Star of David on their clothing. In early 1941, the Romanian authorities initiated a policy of taking Jewish hostages. My mother avoided getting arrested, but her brother and sister were incarcerated. The practice of incarcerating Jews was employed to extract exorbitant ransom payments from the Jewish community. My grandfather attempted to get his children released. The family was most concerned about Uncle David who had several health conditions. Eventually David was released but the police beat my grandfather, and in September 1941, he died at the age of 78 from his injuries.

The Germans handed over to Romania control of the region between the Dniester and Southern Bug rivers (now part of Ukraine), which included the city of Odessa in August 1941. The region was a track of barren and unsettled land, which was called Transnistria, literally meaning "beyond the Dniester River." It didn't even appear on any map at the time. In addition, the Romanian government reached an agreement with Hitler regarding the adoption of the Final Solution, which was firmed up in a meeting with an envoy of Adolf Eichmann in March 1941. In September 1941, Antonescu decided to proceed with the ethnic cleansing of Jews who were now considered an "enemy population," and he set in motion the deportation of Romanian Jews to Transnistria.

On the morning of October 9, 1941, an ordinance was issued in Suceava requiring all Jews to present themselves to the railway station with hand luggage only. Anyone remaining in the town would be shot. My mom's family learned of the evacuation order through drum rolls by the local gendarme, who also distributed pamphlets. This was how edicts were normally announced to the public. Even the sick and elderly were required to leave. The first transport left just hours after the order was delivered. Mom and her family traveled by foot to the Burdujeni railway station outside of Suceava. It was best described as chaos as Mom, her mother, and her two siblings were loaded onto cattle cars, which still had fresh manure on the floor. About 50 people were crammed into each car, and once the doors were shut, they were in complete darkness. There was no food, water, nor toilets. One bucket could be used as a toilet, and it quickly overflowed.

They were instructed not to take any possessions with them except for a small bag, because they were led to believe that they would be returning. My mother regretted not smuggling some valuables, which could have been later traded for food. The train ride lasted about a day. It was too crowded to move, and several people died en route. The living had to stand on the dead who were sprawled on the floors of the cars. When the train arrived at the Volcinet train station on the border with Ukraine, the deportees were removed from the cars while beaten with batons and rifle butts. The dead were dumped in the Dniester River. Mom said they stayed in Ataky for several days, housed in what was left of the destroyed houses in the former Jewish quarter until they were ordered to move again.

8   TRADING SHOES FOR FOOD

My mother and her family were not prepared for what they were to experience when reaching the border with Ukraine. No one was. They were forced to cross the Dniester on rafts. Those who resisted or were unable to walk were shot and thrown into the river. The guards and soldiers accompanying the train would rob the deportees of the few possessions they had. Itzhak Zloczower, mom's oldest brother, and married with children living in Czernowitz, drowned while crossing the Dniester River on a raft.[1] This was likely no accident.

After several days in Ataky, my mother and her family were marched to their destination. Again, those who were unable to walk were shot or left to die. The first stop was Mogilev, which had one of the largest ghettos in Transnistria. In Mogilev, they were taken to filthy barracks without windows, which was used as a central gathering and selection location. However, before reaching the barracks, the Romanians ordered everyone to go through a last-minute search. Any valuables found were confiscated. My mother's family were eventually allowed to leave the barracks to look for shelter. They knocked on the doors of the Jewish ghetto residents, begging the inhabitants to take them in. They resorted to begging for food. My

---

1. Before World War II, the Dniester River was the border between Romania and Ukraine. As a reward for joining the Axis Powers, the Nazis handed over administration of the tract of land between the Dniester and the Bug, to Romania. The territory was called Transnistria and became a massive killing field. Perhaps the closest analogy would be the resettlement of intellectuals in Cambodia under the Khmer Rouge in the 1970s.

mother stole food from pigsties and traded whatever she and her siblings could get their hands on for food.

After several weeks, Mom and her family were once again forced to move by foot, this time to Shargorod. The trip took three days, and they were expected to find their own shelter and food en route. If they couldn't keep up the elderly and sick were left behind to die; the road was lined with the dead from previous convoys of deportees. After three days of plodding from one village to another, they reached Shargorod, another ghetto, where they had to find their own shelter.

Shargorod, once a thriving center for Jewish culture and religious life, was the largest ghetto in Transnistria. Most of the deported Jews from Suceava (about 5,000) were sent to Shargorod, where approximately 2,000 local Jews lived. The Romanian authorities took no responsibility for providing any support, and food distribution was erratic; the Jews in the ghetto were left on their own. Just like in Polish ghettos, a Jewish committee was formed headed by Dr. Meir Teich to distribute what food, clothing, and medical supplies they were able to find. As a result of the work done by Dr. Teich's committee, Shargorod experienced a lower mortality rate than other Transnistria ghettos. Although the place had a Jewish police force, they did not assist the Nazis but defended the Jews from attacks by local non-Jews. The ghetto had 337 small, old clay houses, each with little ventilation, which had to accommodate 7,000 people. Hence, up to 20 people were living in a single room. There were no toilets in Shargorod, which contributed to a typhus outbreak in December 1941; people used the river to relieve themselves. Approximately 4,000 Jews of the Shargorod Ghetto died of typhus.

Almost 80 percent of ghetto residents became infected, including my mother's entire family. Fortunately, the family recovered from the epidemic, while 40 percent of deportees died over the winter. Carts pulled by scrawny horses picked up the dead, who were stripped of their clothes, which were subsequently bartered for food. Burials took place in manually dug mass graves. In the winter, it was impossible to dig graves because the ground was frozen, so the bodies were simply piled up. In the spring, when the corpses thawed, animals would gnaw at the bodies.

Mom's family found a family of Shargorod Jews who reluctantly took them in and gave them a closet in the basement to live in. The basement had a large room with two families and a smaller room with a woman and two children. There was no heating or warm clothing; in the morning my mother would find ice in her hair. People were desperate for food. At one point, Mom traded her shoes for food and wrapped her feet in rags. She would search through people's garbage for food scraps like potato peels and roast them on a fire.

She and her siblings eventually worked odd jobs in exchange for food, such as delivering water to local Jewish families because of the lack of indoor plumbing. Mom found a family who gave her bread in exchange for washing their clothes in the river. There were only four wells in the ghetto to accommodate thousands of people. Another job she acquired was to scrub the inside of a brick oven that was used to bake bread. Over time, she developed a badly infected thumb, which got so bad that she walked 20 kilometers to a small hospital to get it looked at. That put her at risk of being shot because Jews were not allowed to leave the ghetto. Her thumb never properly healed and was permanently deformed.

Although my grandmother recovered from her bout with typhus, she was weak and frail. She lost close to 50 kilograms and developed a twisted bowel. Without medical intervention, she died in December 1943, just four months before they were liberated.

9 DESTRUCTION OF THE JEWS OF BEDZIN

The Nazis convened what became known as the Wannsee Conference on January 20, 1942, at a villa in Berlin's Wannsee suburb. Fifteen senior officials attended. The outcome of that conference was the introduction of the "Final Solution," a euphemism for the Nazi plans for genocide. The conference initiated the mass murder of millions of European Jews, including those from Bedzin. Operation Reinhard was the code name for the German plan to murder the Jews residing in Poland. The operation was named after SS General Reinhard Heydrich, who was a key architect of the Final Solution. To achieve the goals of Operation Reinhard, the Germans constructed four killing centers: Chełmno, Bełzec, Sobibor, and Treblinka. They also expanded Majdanek and Auschwitz-Birkenau to allow them to operate as concentration camps and extermination centers.

Most Jews of Bedzin were deported to Auschwitz-Birkenau which was only a half-hour away. There were three major deportations from Bedzin between 1942 and 1943, during which "unproductive" Jews – those considered too young, too old, or too weak to work – were deported to Auschwitz-Birkenau for gassing. Bedzin Jews were early victims of the newly constructed gas chambers that were first used on Soviet prisoners in September 1941.

The first *Aktion* in Bedzin took place on May 12, 1942, when approximately 3,200 were deported to Auschwitz. These Jews were among the first to be led through a charade where they believed they were being taken to showers; this was done because earlier victims would panic when brought straight to the gas chambers. New arrivals were told to undress in an open field. Eventually, the SS constructed change rooms adjacent to the gas chambers, so that the killings wouldn't be as conspicuous. During the early deportations from Bedzin, word leaked out from Polish railway workers that the trains were going to Auschwitz. As Jews became aware of their plight, resistance increased. Residents ignored requests from the Jewish Council to report for deportation, and some attempted to escape. At the Bedzin collection site, there was considerable panic and violence. Many people were shot trying to resist.

On August 12, 1942, the largest deportation from the region took place. Every Jew in the Bedzin Ghetto was required to report to the Hakoach or the Samacja sports grounds to have their identity cards revalidated. A similar Aktion was taking place in Sosnowiec, to avoid the chaos that occurred in May. The fields were surrounded by armed soldiers who kept the Jews in the sun and overnight in the rain for two days without food and water before the selection began. Each person was called to a table to be examined by an SS official, and those who could not make it on their own were dragged to the stadium by police. A German officer divided people into three groups based on their deemed productivity. One section of the stadium was filled with children and the elderly. Another, with young, healthy men and women. And finally, a third with a mix of people. The first group was sent to Auschwitz-Birkenau and were taken directly to the gas chambers. The second group was sent to the Schmelt forced labor camps. The third group was eventually sent back to their homes. This group included those who had a blue work identity card (such as those who worked for Alfred Rossner). My aunt Machela and the seven children under her care were spared for another year. My two cousins' blue work identity cards provided then with a temporary reprieve from deportation. The operation involved 23,000 people and resulted in about 4,700 Bedzin Ghetto residents being selected for deportation. Despite the SS ruse where identity cards were being validated, the Aktion got so out of control at one point that riots broke out. Hundreds were shot trying to escape before being put on the trains. Future deportation would require forcibly removing Jews from their homes to be taken to the train station. The ghetto had finally become a form of incarceration.

By July 1943, the Jews of Bedzin were becoming increasingly aware of their intended fate and were attempting to avoid deportation. Eventually, the Jewish Council was no longer able to convince Jewish residents to appear for deportation, and the SS and Gestapo took over the task of rounding them up. In fact, the Bedzin Judenrat had been sent to Auschwitz the previous month, a signal to the remaining residents of what was to come.

Resistance continued to grow for those still in the ghetto. Following the Warsaw Ghetto uprising in spring 1943, there was increased interest in armed resistance, and weapons were smuggled into the Bedzin Ghetto. The Germans were concerned about further uprisings. They tightened control over the ghetto by restricting movement further. The most significant act of resistance was hiding during the forced deportation actions. The residents built hiding places in false floors, inside large cupboards, behind false walls in cellars, under trapdoors in gardens and yards, and in the rafters of attics – wherever a few bodies could squeeze. But these hiding places provided only temporary escape from deportation, as there were no food, water, or sanitation facilities for those hidden.

Machela also built a hiding place for her family. Behind the stove they constructed a partition, six feet by eight feet, which was hidden by a curtain above the stove. A second hiding place was required because they couldn't all fit in. Because the house had a dirt floor, they were able to create a smaller hiding place by digging under the bed.

In 1943, Himmler dismantled the Schmelt Organization. The Warsaw ghetto uprising seems to have convinced Himmler that it was time to move forward with their extermination policy. The last major deportations from Bedzin took place on August 1, 1943. The deportation began at 4 a.m. with SS and Gestapo personnel dragging people out of their homes to the main square in the ghetto. Those who had bunkers hid to avoid the roundup. The Germans went from home to home, searching for hiding places and firing into walls and attics. Even workers from Rossner's shops were included in the Aktion. This was intended to be the final deportation of Jews from Bedzin, making it *Judenrein* [cleansed of Jews]. The Aktion lasted for four days and resulted in the expulsion of 12,000 Jews from Bedzin and Sosnowiec. Some died in their bunkers under horrible conditions. Those in hiding eventually needed to leave for food and water. Most were captured, and they were either shot or sent to Auschwitz.

Machela and the children were among the final group to be deported to Auschwitz-Birkenau in August 1943. For nine days, they had avoided the deportation order by remaining in their hiding places. They could hear shouting and shots throughout the day and night. Occasionally they would peek outside and see dead bodies and personal possessions littering the streets. They survived on raw potatoes and drank their own urine because there was no water. Eventually, they had to leave their hiding places and were immediately arrested by the SS, who had them transported to Auschwitz-Birkenau.

The Germans reported that some 2,800 people were shot while "trying to escape." The ghetto was finally cleared of the remaining Jewish residents during the August 1943 deportation. About 1,000 remaining Jews were deported in the subsequent months. In February 1944, the last 200 Bedzin Jews were forced to clean up the ghetto, which included pulling out the remaining bodies from the rubble. After the job was completed, they too were sent to Auschwitz. There were no Jews left in Bedzin except for small numbers that were being hidden by Poles.

10 DAD'S FIRST FAMILY

One of the fuzzier parts of my father's past was his first family. He told us that the Nazis killed his first wife, Estera, and four-year-old daughter, Laja. Just mentioning their names brought him to tears. I didn't know when he married or when Laja was born, but I assumed both took place before start of the war. I never asked because it was obviously too painful to talk about. I also never asked about the circumstance in which they died. When I received a package of scanned documents from the Arolsen Archives in late 2021, they included my dad's Buchenwald prisoner registration form dated February 10, 1945. The form indicated that he had two children (ages two and four years old) but provided no names. It was my understanding that my father had just one daughter. While the handwritten card caught my attention, I assumed it was an error and didn't give it any further thought. From the registration card, I learned that his wife's maiden name was Sledzik, which allowed me to search for information using her family name.

A few months later I received information that had me shaking. I had already received birth, death, and marriage records from Jewish Records Indexing (JRI) Poland for the Oksenhendler family in Wislica. That information helped me assemble a family tree. I decided to also request any family records that were archived in Bedzin. I didn't expect much information because the family had only lived in Bedzin for about a dozen years. JRI Poland sent me several spreadsheets extracted from records with the surname Oksenhendler. One spreadsheet indicated my father and Estera were married in 1940. Another spreadsheet indicated they had registered the birth of two children: Laja, born in 1940, and Jenta, born in 1941. It turned out that the Buchenwald record was correct.

I was stunned to learn that my dad had a second daughter. I couldn't understand why he had never mentioned her. My first thought was that he wasn't aware that he had a second daughter. I reasoned that maybe she was born after he was deported from Bedzin. But slowly I uncovered information suggesting that he did know.

Some time later, I retrieved a box of old family photos from my sister that she had been holding onto after my parents passed away. It took me considerable time to identify several people in the photos. There was one photo that caught me by surprise. It included my grandmother and two of her daughters (Jentla and Mariem), as well as my father's first wife (Estera), and their two daughters (Jenta and Laja). The younger one, Jenta, looked so much like her mother. The girls appeared to be about one and two years old in the photo. Now I had faces to match the names. I don't know how the photo survived the Holocaust or how my father got hold of it. I am sure the photo was taken in the summer of 1942 after my father was deported from the Bedzin Ghetto, based on the ages of the girls and the weather. Oddly enough, my father had never mentioned Jenta to his second family. He had this photo but had not shared it with any of us. It had just collected dust in a shoebox. I'm quite positive that not even my mother knew. There were sleepless nights as I tried to make sense of this information. No one just forgets that they had a second child. The Buchenwald record was dated February 10, 1945. It listed the girls' ages, but they couldn't have still been alive in 1945. Dad had no idea what their fate had been.

What I determined was that my father married Estera Sledzik, the sister-in-law of his older sister, Jentla. Estera's family was from Pinczow and had moved to Bedzin several years before the start of the war. They met before the war and were married before a rabbi in 1940, the same year that Laja was born. Jenta was born a year later.

I was also able to determine that during the selection and mass deportation that took place in Bedzin Ghetto on August 12, 1942, my grandparents, Estera, Laja, and Jenta were shipped by train to Auschwitz-Birkenau. I was able to confirm the timing with my cousin Jadzia who witnessed and survived that selection.

My poor family was unloaded on a newly built platform between Auschwitz I (the Main Camp) and Auschwitz II (the Birkenau killing center) for a selection. They were most probably led to a provisional gas chamber in a former farmhouse. At the time, the SS camp administration was still in the process of building integrated gas chambers and crematoria. As a result, the bodies of the victims were dumped into a pit. The only time my half-sisters left the ghetto was to travel in a cattle car to Birkenau. The girls never got to experience things like eating an ice cream cone, going to the movies, or falling in love. Their last experience was hearing the screams of the victims in the gas chamber. It was not unusual for children to be crushed by panicking adults trying to avoid the gas. It breaks my heart every time I think about it. These images continue to haunt me.

As I grew up, I began to understand that my mom, my siblings and I were a replacement family. My father's priority following the war was to remarry and have children, but he had not moved forward from the death of this first family and was stuck in the process of grieving. We were meant to fill a void that my father hadn't healed from. He experienced a lot of trauma throughout his life and was emotionally unavailable to us. As a replacement child, I have experienced a lifetime of existential anxiety, feeling unseen or unheard, guilt, and ill at ease with life. However, none of this compares to the grief that my father has passed on to me.

11 SONDERKOMMANDO

Dad had many bad experiences in the camps, but the worst must have been his brief time as a *Sonderkommando*. Sonderkommando is German word for "special command unit," but it had a rather different meaning in the context of concentration camps. I don't remember how old I was when he told me about this period of the war, but the revelation was so upsetting. It might have been when I first had nightmares.

Sonderkommandos were forced to assist with the murder of Jews, among them many elderly and women with children. I can't imagine what that must have been like. Knowing that your own wife, children, and parents might have experienced the same fate. Sonderkommandos understood that they would eventually be joining the naked pile of lifeless bodies.

The final months of the war were the worst for my dad. He wasn't sure he would survive. At Fünfteichen the prisoners realized that during the final weeks of 1944, the war would be ending based on the number of air raids. There were no bomb shelters for the prisoners who dove into trenches that were just a meter deep outside the barracks. The evacuation of Fünfteichen began on January 21, 1945, some were evacuated by rail but most on foot. Prisoners were sent to the main Gross-Rosen camp located near what is now Rogoznica, Poland. My father was transferred to Gross-Rosen early that month and missed the four-day death march by about two weeks. Prisoners were often placed in Gross-Rosen for transfer to one of the subcamps, but near the end of the war the movement of prisoners was back to the main camp. Dad was transferred on a train transport which was also risky because the rail lines were being bombed by the Allies.

Gross-Rosen was by far the worst of the camps my father experienced. The forced labor camps were bad enough, but at least prisoners who worked hard and followed the rules might somehow survive. Deprivation and death were everywhere. Rotting corpses were piled up. My father was only there for about one month and fortunate to have survived the experience. Gross-Rosen had a reputation for its brutal treatment of prisoners, especially those assigned to work in the nearby stone quarry. The average life expectancy was only two months. Thousands died of starvation, while others didn't survive the beatings that were regularly doled out at the quarry whenever prisoners weren't "working hard enough." My dad was not given a factory job or sent to work in the quarry but worked as a Sonderkommando. Because the camp had no gas chamber, he was not involved in the extermination of prisoners. Each night, prisoners died of exhaustion, disease, or physical abuse. The bodies were removed from the bunks in the morning to be cremated. In some cases, prisoners too weak to work in the stone quarry were given a lethal injection and sent to the crematorium. The camp had a field crematorium until a permanent brick structure was built to dispose of the bodies. During the time that my father was in Gross-Rosen, he worked at the permanent crematorium.

Sonderkommandos lived in separate quarters and kept away from the rest of the camp population. Being assigned to be a Sonderkommando was a death sentence, as they were replaced every few months and subsequently killed. The Nazis did not want any living witnesses to genocide. My father was one of a small number that survived the war. My father had hidden three diamonds that he had found among confiscated property of prisoners. He kept them safely hidden should he need them. One of those diamonds was evidently used to bribe a guard who tipped off my father when it was time to replace him and the other Sonderkommandos in his group. So Dad hid among dead bodies for three days – too terrified to come out. Uncle Israel, who was also at Gross-Rosen at the time, was able to get some stale bread to him to keep him alive. I can't even visualize what it must have been like to be hiding with corpses. As appalling as this story is, it also speaks to how miraculous it was that my father survived and that he would not accept his fate. When he finally came out of hiding, he joined a group of prisoners that were sent to Buchenwald near Weimar, Germany.

The evacuation of Gross-Rosen began in early February 1945, and yet again, my dad managed to avoid the death march. The Germans forced many of the remaining 27,000 prisoners to march to various camps in Germany. My father was included in the initial transfers who were transported by train in open freight cars. It was winter and hundreds died of exposure. Prisoners were being moved to camps deeper in Germany as the Russian forces marched through Poland.

A transport list indicated that he was sent to Buchenwald on February 10, 1945. He had been examined by a camp doctor in Buchenwald on February 17, 1945, and was subsequently assigned light work. Each day, he was taken by rail to Weimar to work in a Krupp munitions factory. Although he escaped certain death at Gross-Rosen, he would never be the same after this experience. Even one month burning corpses will mess you up the rest of your life.

12 ANGEL OF DEATH

When my aunt Machela and her children arrived at Birkenau, they were immediately put through a selection on the train platform overseen by Dr. Josef Mengele. Mengele was the chief physician at Birkenau, and he was frequently involved in the selection of prisoners to be sent to the gas chambers. He was referred to in Hebrew as the *Mal'ach Ha'Mavett*, the "Angel of Death." It was a frightening scene with heavily armed SS guards and vicious dogs. Military trucks were parked next to the train platform that would later be used to transport the elderly and children to Crematorium III and its connected gas chamber. The SS showed no mercy, no compassion or emotion as they systematically processed their victims.

Lemel, who was her youngest, was separated from the rest of the family along with two younger cousins during the selection process on the train platform. Machela had told him to line up with the men. However, the officer in charge directed him to join a group of children that were being loaded onto a truck. Following his mother's instructions, he kept sneaking back to the men's group. The SS would pull him out of the line and send him back with the other children. This was repeated several times until he was last seen being driven off in a dump truck filled with children headed to the gas chambers. His mother and sister could do nothing but watch helplessly. It was the last time they saw him, and they carried around this profound loss for the rest of their lives.

It is estimated that of the 30,000 inhabitants of the ghetto, less that 2,000 survived the war. Auschwitz-Birkenau kept no records of those who were separated by camp officials upon arrival and murdered. They understood those records could one day be used against them. Those who survived the initial selection on the railway station platform at Birkenau were registered. The intake process at Birkenau was dehumanizing and humiliating. My cousin Regina described how they were stripped naked in one barrack, and their clothes taken away. They were marched naked to other barracks where all body hair was shaved off by a male prisoner. They were then handed an ill-fitting striped prison dress with a pair of uncomfortable wooden shoes, but no underwear. Along with the clothing was a small enamel bowl which they learned was needed to get food. Finally, their camp number was tattooed onto their left forearm. My aunt and her daughters were numbers 54090, 54091, and 54092. Finally, the three were taken to a lice-infested block 20, their new home for the next 17 months.

My aunt and two cousins survived through the resourcefulness of Machela. They learned to prick their fingers and rub blood into their cheeks prior to roll calls so that they wouldn't appear as pale and sickly. My cousin Jadzia was 16 when she arrived at Auschwitz-Birkenau. She had lost her left arm prior to the war in an accident. When the family first arrived at Auschwitz-Birkenau, Machela had a large shawl draped around her shoulders which she used to cover up Jadzia's missing arm.

The subsequent 17 months was a cat and mouse game to avoid being noticed by the SS officers. A common practice for concentration camp survivors was to avoid standing out or being noticed. Obscurity was important to survival and Jenny became quite good at it. During the roll calls twice a day, Machela would crowd in next to her and concealed her missing arm. During selections, Jadzia would sometimes slip away to hide in another block. Jadzia being a gifted singer likely contributed to her survival at Auschwitz. She entertained the women in her block, keeping their spirits up and in return, they protected her. After the war she continued singing at charitable events, radio shows, and family gatherings, including my wedding.

There was one frightening encounter with Dr. Mengele involving Jadzia. Jadzia was working in the delousing and disinfection building, which was created in December 1943, to control the spread of typhus. Dr. Mengele showed up unannounced to conduct a selection of female prisoners. When he was done, he returned to his car and realized that he had left his briefcase in the building. Mengele sent a female prisoner who was serving as his aide to go back and get it. But instead of grabbing the briefcase, she asked Jadzia to bring it out to the car. The woman explained that she did not want to be blamed if something was missing from the briefcase. Naively, Jadzia walked out with the woman and handed over the briefcase. After Jadzia left, Mengele realized that there was something unusual about her. He asked the aide whether the girl had only one arm. The woman said no, and they drove off. Later, the woman returned and slapped Jadzia across the face. She was livid that Jadzia had put them both in danger of being killed. It was remarkable that she survived over a year in the camp with her impairment. In the fall of 2024 Jadzia turned 97. She was the only remaining survivor in my family.

When Regina contracted dysentery, Machela traded food for coal because it was believed to be a remedy. Regina eventually contracted typhus and was sent to the infirmary where she went into a coma. Most people never returned from the infirmary and ended up in a gas chamber. She eventually recovered and, during her time in the infirmary, was told that Mengele would be coming to conduct a selection that day. Someone handed her some red tissue paper which she wetted and rubbed onto her cheeks to give them some color. She managed to survive the selection and rejoined her mother and sister in their barracks. Another time, Regina was told that she was selected by a German industrialist to work in his factory in Germany. Machela and Jadzia gave up three days of bread rations to have Regina's name removed from the transfer list. Instead, she was transferred from Birkenau to Auschwitz for the remainder of the war. They were no longer together but at least still in the same complex. And conditions in Auschwitz were slightly better than Birkenau with brick barracks and water in the latrines.

13 RESILIENCE AND RESISTANCE

My parents and their survivor friends would describe how they survived such inhumane conditions in the camps. The most common explanation was "luck." No doubt, luck was an element for many survivors, but it didn't fully explain how they stayed alive for so many years under such horrible conditions. Every day camp prisoners made choices without fully understanding what the implications would be. Volunteering for or avoiding a work assignment, not being selected for extermination – there was much more to surviving than just luck. One also needed to be strategic by avoiding situations that could be catastrophic. Associated with the trauma that victims were subjected to, was such incredible resilience.

My father managed to get assigned work in factories in five of the seven camps in which he was held. He largely avoided the more dangerous or physical jobs. I know my father would have done anything to improve his chances of living. He bribed people to get the easier work assignments using whatever he could get his hands on for currency, whether it was stolen property or boots from the dead. His claim of somehow acquiring three diamonds reinforces my belief that one could improve your chances of surviving. He would curry favor with the guards for extra food rations. He also repeatedly avoided death marches in 1945 as concentration camps were evacuated before they were liberated by the advancing Allied. He missed the Fünfteichen death marches by two weeks, the Gross-Rosen death marches by only days, and the Buchenwald death marches by four weeks. Even at his final camp, Bisingen, he was left behind when the camp was evacuated. I don't know how he avoided the death marches, but I don't believe it was entirely through luck.

Those who were capable of working were useful to the Nazis and were kept alive to serve as forced labor. Prisoners were also employed in coal mines and rock quarries, and on construction projects, digging tunnels and canals. Many forced laborers eventually were used in factories that produced weapons and various goods that supported the German war effort. Even at Auschwitz prisoners were assigned work. There were several factories associated with Auschwitz, such as one owned by I.G. Farben. Women often sorted the piles of shoes, clothes, and other prisoner belongings, which would be shipped back to Germany to be used there. The storage warehouses at Auschwitz-Birkenau were called "Kanada," because the Poles regarded Canada as a place of great riches. My cousin Regina worked there while she was in Birkenau. One day she was cold and asked a guard permission to put on a coat from one of the piles to stay warm. He gave his approval and she put one on. When she slipped her hands into the pockets, she could feel something inside the lining. It turned out to be a man's wedding band, with an initial and the wedding date. She smuggled the ring out in her shoe and kept if for the remainder of the war. When she and Barek Eisenstein married, she gave him the ring.

Those who were too old, too young, or in poor health were quickly disposed of. These selections were a clear message on how to survive. One needed to be resilient and adaptable. This applied not just to concentration camp life, but also to those living in the ghettos, those in hiding, and partisans who were part of the Jewish resistance movement. Anyone who lost the will to live likely perished soon after. In the camps, death came quickly to those who had given up. Some chose to take their own lives. The most common form of suicide was to touch the electrified fences found on the camp perimeters.

Those who were separated from family and on their own in the camps had a tougher time and were less likely to survive. People looked after each other, even with the smallest of gestures, such as sharing a piece of bread or some clothing. Except for the last month of the war, my father was always with his brother Israel. They made sure they had enough food, cared for each other after a beating, or just provided the moral support needed to get through the worst days.

I've often heard people ask why the Jewish people gave in to the Nazis without resisting? In most cases, it was because civilians were unarmed. Those who resisted in any way were shot on the spot. Often, the Nazis used deception and a series of lies to get people to cooperate. The Nazis would collect a group of men and inform them there were being taken to a work site, only to be taken into the woods and shot. They would order ghetto residents to report at a collection point to have identity papers validated, and it would turn out to be a selection for deportation. Those sent to concentration camps were told they were just being resettled. They were told to bring along belongings to support this Nazi fiction. At the concentration camps, newly arriving Jews were led into gas chambers that were made to look like showers. They were even asked to neatly fold their clothes or to remember the hook where their clothes would be found once they finished showering. Some fled when the Nazis invaded to join the underground or partisan groups. Escape from camps such as Auschwitz was almost impossible. Electrically charged barbed wire fences surrounded both the concentration camp and the killing center. Guards, equipped with machine guns and automatic rifles, stood guard in watchtowers. There were 928 escapes from Auschwitz, but most were caught and hung in front the camp prisoners at an Appell. There were only 196 successful escapes. Often, other prisoners were shot as a reprisal for those who attempted to escape. And where would an escaped prisoner go when the surrounding inhabitants were hostile? I don't think it's always acknowledged that the most effective form of resistance was staying alive – not losing the will to live. In a way, each survivor did their part to undermine Hitler's plan to destroy European Jewry.

Fighting back was also in the form of cultural, religious, and spiritual resistance. Religious practices were banned in ghettos and camps. Prisoners found ways to celebrate holidays and their culture in secret. At Theresienstadt someone stole a large block of wood and used it to carve an ornate Hanukkah menorah. In Bergen-Belsen 11 survivors saved scraps of fat from their food and used loose threads to form makeshift wicks for a menorah. In the Toronto Holocaust Museum there is a handmade calendar that logs each Jewish date and weekly Torah *parsha* [portion] for the Jewish year of 1944-45, which was carried around by someone in Theresienstadt. Shlomo Ullmann and Mordecai Glick wrote a prayer book for Rosh Hashanah and *Yom Kippur* [Day of Atonement] from memory when they were interned in a POW camp in Siberia in 1944. Mordecai wrote them down on pages of Soviet propaganda, printed on tobacco leaves, which Shlomo took from the infirmary. People risked their lives during the Holocaust to keep their traditions alive.

There were several uprisings in ghettos and concentration camps. The best-known uprising took place in the Warsaw Ghetto, which began on April 19,

1943 when the Nazis entered the ghetto to deport the remaining inhabitants. Jewish resistance was led by about 700 young Jewish fighters who were armed with smuggled weapons. Resistance lasted 27 days as the SS troops were forced to raze the ghetto, block by block. Approximately 13,000 Jews were killed during the uprising. Half of the victims were burned or suffocated in the fires. The remainder were shot by the Nazi troops. The SS reported about 110 German casualties in the Warsaw Ghetto uprising. Although the number of German deaths were low, the uprising was a major concern for the Nazis who accelerated the liquidation of ghettos to avoid further uprisings.

Yet, there were uprisings in other ghettos. In Bedzin, a similar uprising took place, beginning on August 3, 1943, when the SS initiated the final liquidation of the ghetto. Resistance was organized by a woman, Fumia Płotnicka, who escaped the Warsaw Ghetto following their uprising. Płotnicka used false identities to travel across Nazi-occupied Poland as a courier, delivering guns and instructions for building weapons to underground Jewish groups. The Bedzin Ghetto uprising involved about 1,400 Jews and lasted three days until the fighters ran out of ammunition. SS units sent from Auschwitz destroyed the bunker that housed Płotnicka and the other insurgents, killing them all. The captured uprising survivors were transported to Auschwitz but did not go through the usual selection process. They were shot and killed on the train platform because the SS was concerned about further resistance. When I visited Bedzin in August 2022, I was taken to the site of the bunker on Podsiadly Street in the former ghetto. There was a memorial plaque on the building that led to the bunker.

On October 14, 1943, prisoners in Sobibor killed 11 SS guards and police auxiliaries and set the camp on fire. About 300 prisoners escaped, breaking through the barbed wire, risking their lives in the minefield surrounding the camp. Over 100 were recaptured and later shot. From those that successfully escaped, only 50 survived.

On October 7, 1944, the largest Auschwitz uprising and escape took place, led by a group of Sonderkommandos. It was a carefully thought-out plan that overcame incredible logistical odds. Some of the key players were female Jewish prisoners from Bedzin who worked at Weichsel-Union-Metallwerke, a munitions factory within the Auschwitz complex. In the months leading up to the October uprising, these women had painstakingly smuggled tiny quantities of gunpowder from the factory and delivered them to the Auschwitz underground. The female smugglers used ingenious techniques, hiding tiny amounts of powder in folds of their clothing or in body cavities as they were searched daily by SS guards. One woman smuggled out a pair of rubber-handled shears that would later be used to cut the electric fence as part of an escape attempt. The smuggled material was passed on to a Russian munition expert, who prepared makeshift bombs and grenades. My cousin Regina was close friends with one the smugglers from Bedzin, Regina Safirsztain.

On the day of the uprising word leaked that 300 Sonderkommandos were to be killed and replaced. Prisoners in Gas Chamber IV killed the SS leader with hammers and set fire to the Crematorium IV. The attack was supposed to be coordinated with those working at the other Birkenau crematoria. The attempt to blow up the equipment was only partially successful. What followed was chaos. The SS found themselves attacked on all sides by prisoners, brandishing hammers, knives, and explosive devices. One SS guard who was noted for extreme cruelty was thrown into a crematorium oven alive. Some of the prisoners also cut their way through the electric fence using the stolen shears to flee into the woods, while the SS opened fire with machine guns. The Germans immediately sent for reinforcements and quickly quelled the rebellion. All escapees were captured and killed. About 250 Jews died during the uprising. The SS lined up another 200 prisoners and shot them as a reprisal for the rebellion. The SS lost three men, with about ten wounded.

My cousin recalls that the Germans searched the blocks following the uprising looking for additional gunpowder. They took each bunk apart. The Germans managed to identify four of the female conspirators, who worked in the munition factory. The women were tortured for an extended period but only provided the SS with names of people who had perished in the uprising. They were hung on January 5, 1945 in front of the assembled women's camp, which Regina witnessed. It was just three weeks before the liberation of Auschwitz.

For most, resistance was pointless, and survival was paramount. Every decision made was based on whether it would help them survive. They had to suppress the trauma and brutality they were experiencing, the hunger that gnawed at them, their fears and anxiety, and images of death and the atrocities around them. They witnessed parents and children being killed. Some were assigned gruesome jobs such as loading bodies into the crematoriums or extracting gold teeth from the mouths of the deceased. They had to endure difficult physical labor – such as working in stone quarries, with little food, harsh winters with no warm clothing – and widespread diseases that swept through the camps. Whether it was my dad courting favor from a camp guard for an extra ration of stale bread or my mom searching through garbage for food scraps to eat, this is where their resilience came from and continued after liberation. I saw the resilience in my parents. Their focus was always on surviving and not necessarily on enjoying life. Pleasure came from their children and grandchildren because we replaced the family they had lost. It is an enormous burden on children.

14 OKSENHENDLER FAMILY SURVIVORS

My father's stay in Buchenwald was also quite short. In March 1945 he was transferred for the last time. The frequent moves were intended to avoid handing over prisoners who had witnessed war crimes to the Allied troops. At this point of the war, the German army was in full retreat while the top brass continuing to focus on finishing off what was left of European Jewry. His last camp was Bisingen, a subcamp of the Natzweiler-Struthof concentration camp network. The camp was in southwest Germany near the city of Konstanz and about 160 kilometers from the French border. The Germans moved prisoners to priority work locations despite knowing that the war was lost.

He never mentioned his time in Bisingen, but it was part of the wartime record I received from the Arolsen Archives. I received a transport list indicating he had been transferred from Buchenwald to Bisingen March 5, 1945, to work on a secret project. Towards the end of the war, the Germans were running low on vital supplies, especially fuel, and were looking for alternative sources of oil. The project's code name was *Unternehmen Wuste* [Operation Desert], and in fact, one of the documents I received indicated my father was sent to the camp on such a transport. The first shale plant had only gone into production two weeks prior to his arrival.

Prisoners chipped away at the shale with hammers from quarries close to the camp. The prisoners then shoveled the crushed shale into a trench where it was ignited. The theory was that the warm shale would release oil, but the process produced the smallest amounts of useable oil. The project was a failure because of poor technology and the high death rate among the prisoners. The camp *Kommandant* [commander] was eventually removed from his position when it was learned that he was secretly adding oil to the shale slags to keep the project alive.

According to his reparation application Dad was assigned to work in the plant instead of the back-breaking shale quarries. Since the camp had no crematorium the dead were dumped into an open pit. One of the factors that contributed to his survival is that, except for the Rattwitz and Gross-Rosen concentration camps, he was always assigned factory work. This was safer and less physically taxing than work in quarries or road construction and without exposure to extreme weather. I don't believe this was entirely by luck. Dad was the type who would appeal for lighter work and provide bribes if he were in the position to do so. He was heavily involved in the black markets that operated in the camps and bartered or bribed people to make his life easier. He claimed to have acquired three diamonds that he used to keep himself safe. Currency in the camps ranged from bread ration to cigarettes, but other contraband was used as well. Many guards and Kapos were corrupt and could be bought off.

When Allied troops approached Bisingen in April 1945, the Nazis evacuated the camp. About 700 prisoners were sent on a death march to Dachau. Dad again avoided the death march, although I don't know how. He was still in the camp when it was liberated by the French First Army on April 20, 1945. These camp evacuations were chaotic. It was less than three weeks before Germany surrendered. The Germans scrambled to destroy evidence of their crimes by burning files and destroying gas chambers and crematoriums. During this bedlam, my father would have had an opportunity to hide and avoid the evacuation.

I can imagine the shock experienced by Allied soldiers when they arrived at the camp to find dead bodies piled up everywhere. The living looked much the same as the dead. They were lice-ridden skeletons with sunken eyes, covered in dirt. The French forces ordered the mass grave at Bisingen to be exhumed, and the victims were given proper burial in a cemetery built specifically to accommodate those killed at the camp.

Even after liberation prisoners continued to die from typhus, tuberculosis, or general ill health. Many prisoners were near death when the Allied troops arrived, having not been fed in days. The liberating troops handed out food, organized the burial of the dead, and sent those in the worst condition to hospitals to convalesce. My father said he barely ate when offered food. He noticed some survivors died because their digestive systems couldn't handle the food. Dad weighed under 45 kilograms when he left Bisingen concentration camp after years of living on starvation diets while performing up to 12 hours of physical labor every day.

Other family members had a challenging time re-establishing their lives. They left the camps with countless physical and mental conditions. Uncle Moishe was initially sent to several different subcamps of Auschwitz, including Greiditz and Lautahutte, where he was given construction work. He was transferred to several additional forced labor camps, including Gross Panuf, Brande, Kittlitzstreben (a Gross-Rosen subcamp), and ended the war in Buchenwald from which where he was liberated by the US Third Army on April 11, 1945. Before the war he had trained to be a tailor to help support the family, and in the camps he often found work mending uniforms for the Germans. He had incurred numerous beatings and had lost significant hearing. He evaded the death marches out of Buchenwald by hiding under floorboards in a barracks. Following liberation, the Allied troops transferred him to Sweden for treatment of a broken leg that had become badly infected. He remained in Sweden until he and his family emigrated to Canada in 1950.

His wife Machela and daughter Jadzia were forced to go on a death march in January 1945 when the Nazis evacuated Auschwitz-Birkenau. They were fortunate in that they only marched to a train station in Wodzisław where they were crammed into freight trains and transported to Ravensbrück. In some cases, prisoners were marched much further. The longest march was to Gross-Rosen concentration camp, about 275 kilometers. The Auschwitz prisoners were informed on January 17 that the camp was being evacuated. The evacuation took place between January 17 and January 21, during blizzard conditions and subfreezing temperatures. About 58,000 prisoners from Auschwitz and its neighboring subcamps were forced to leave. These camp evacuations become known as death marches because thousands of prisoners perished along the way. The number of Auschwitz prisoners that died during the evacuation is estimated to be about 15,000 or about 25 percent of those that were forced out of the camp.

Between January 20 and 26, the SS blew up the buildings housing the gas chambers and crematoria. Some 9,000 prisoners were left by the SS in the camps because they were either dying or too ill to be evacuated. Some healthier prisoners avoided the death march by hiding. My cousin Regina was one of them. She hid with four other prisoners in a basement of barracks for five days. They eventually joined several men in the Auschwitz underground who also went into hiding. This group included Barek Eisenstein, who Regina would later marry. She was liberated by the Red Army soldiers from the 322nd Rifle Division on January 27, 1945. When the Russians arrived only 7,000 prisoners were still alive. Two thousand had died in the time between the Germans leaving and the Russians arriving at the camp, and more would expire in the subsequent days and weeks.

Uncle Israel had spent much of the war with my dad. They were together in Ottmuth, Rattwitz, Markstädt, Fünfteichen, Gross-Rosen, and Buchenwald. Israel ended the war in Theresienstadt which is now in the Czech Republic. I have seen many photos and newsreels of liberated concentration camp prisoners. Many were walking skeletons. These photos were difficult to look at, but the victims were anonymous, which mitigated the emotional response. I had never seen a photo of a family member immediately following liberation until late 2023. My cousin Jadzia shared a photo of Israel immediately after liberation. He was still in his camp uniform that hung on his emaciated and tuberculosis-ridden body. He had a haggard look and was hunched over. He was 35 years old in the photo but looked almost double that age. After the war, he was sent to the Gauting Sanitorium for Displaced Persons in Germany, where he underwent treatment for tuberculosis. He settled in Munich where he met and married Dora Ratgerber. They had two children and immigrated to Toronto in the 1960s. I learned that his tuberculosis diagnosis made it impossible to immigrate until the restriction was lifted.

In 1941 Aunt Sara was sent to Bernsdorf, a textile forced labor camp for women and a subcamp of Gross-Rosen in what is now the Czech Republic. She also finished the war in Theresienstadt. Following the war, she settled in Munich where she met and married Moritz Secemski. They emigrated to Israel in the early 1950s and had three children.

15 ZLOCZOWER FAMILY SURVIVORS

Following the end of World War I, Mom's two oldest sisters left Romania. Mary immigrated to the United States and settled in New York City in December 1920. She was unhappy with life in Romania where antisemitism and attacks on Jews were becoming more frequent. Mary was sponsored by my grandfather's brother, Isak Zloczower, who arrived in the US in 1897 with his wife Eva and seven children. When Mary arrived, she had difficulty contacting Isak, and immigration authorities were prepared to send her back to Europe. She eventually discovered that Isak and the family had changed their surname to Schlosser. Mary was finally connected with Isak and was allowed to remain in New York. Isak and Eva had two additional children after they arrived in New York. My mother's sister, Ruth, followed Mary to New York in November 1923. My aunts also changed their surnames to Schlosser shortly after arriving in America.

Over the years, the contingent of Zlocowers/Schlossers in the New York area grew considerably. As is the case with many large families, they weren't all close. When I visited New York in the 1950s and 1960s, I only met my uncles and aunts. In the early years, the family lived in the Lower East Side of Manhattan in tenement buildings. Immigrant Jews started out with pushcarts or worked in the garment industry. That certainly was the experience for the Schlosser family. I tracked down one of the grandsons of Isak and Eva Schlosser and had a few conversations with him. He identified some family members in photos that were left to us by my aunt Mary. He had little contact with his extended family and didn't know the names of his father's eight siblings.

Mary and Ruth lived for some time with their cousin, Abe Schlosser (one of Isak and Eva's sons) and his wife, Fannie. Mary was close with her cousin Abe, who owned a candy store where Mary worked until she married. Ruth worked in a clothing factory designing dresses. She was a talented designer, and in the photos I have of Ruth, she typically was stylishly dressed. Mary met an American, Ruby Michaels, and they married in 1932. Ruth had health issues and never married. She had a stroke at an early age that left her impaired. Sadly, she took her own life in the 1950s. Ruth went back to visit the family in Comanesti in the 1930s. She took numerous photos of the family and their home, which I now possess.

The war years were very stressful for my aunts as they lost contact with family. My mother didn't meet her oldest sister until after the war, when Mary visited my mother and her other siblings in Israel in 1949.

Two brothers, Srul and Joshua, were conscripted into the Romanian army in the 1930s. Joshua was a committed Zionist with a strong desire to resettle in Palestine. In 1934, while on leave in Bucharest, he deserted from the army and left for Palestine by ship. Romanian Government authorities contacted the family on numerous occasions, looking for him but they denied knowing his whereabouts.

While during research for my memoir I learned that my maternal grandfather received a proper burial following his death in 1941. Someone provided me with a photo of his gravestone which still exists in a neglected and overgrown Suceava cemetery. The gravestone has the inscription on the bottom that reads: "Wolf Zloczower, Komanesti." The Hebrew inscription states he is Zev (his Hebrew name), son of Tzvi Nissan (my great-grandfather's Hebrew name). It also states that he died on the Hebrew date of Elul 14, which fell on September 6, 1941. My grandfather is the only Holocaust victim in the family who has an actual grave.

For my mother, incarceration ended before the conclusion of the war in Europe for. Early in 1944 rumors spread that the German and Romanian troops were planning to withdraw from Transnistria to avoid the advancing Russian Army. The Shargorod Ghetto inhabitants could hear bombing during the first few weeks of March. On March 20, 1944, a Russian cavalry unit arrived to liberate the ghetto. Most surviving Jews left Transnistria after warnings that it would not be safe to stay under Soviet rule. Mom and her siblings were too frightened to leave, as were some of the other deportees. They felt it would not be safe to return to Romania because of concerns about lingering antisemitism. Many had been subjected to pogroms before being deported to Transnistria.

In August 1944 Antonescu's government was overthrown by an antifascist group called the National Democratic Bloc. The new government signed an agreement with the Soviet Union that formally acknowledged that Romania was no longer allied with Germany. Antonescu was arrested and, after the war, convicted of war crimes and hung.

When the Russians tried to send my mother and her siblings to work in the coal mines in the Donbass region of Ukraine, they decided it was time to leave. In early 1945 they returned to Suceava. Because many of the returning residents had been back for a year, they had already established themselves and were active in the thriving black market. Mom, Rachel, and David made money taking on odd jobs. They had become disillusioned with Romania, as had many Jews, and were ready to move on. The communists had control of the country and had shut down or restricted the activities of Zionist and other Jewish organizations.

Mom, Rachel, and David decided to emigrate to Palestine, which was the destination of choice for the majority of surviving Romanian Jews. Mom had saved two gold pieces that were given to her by a woman who had employed her in Shargorod to bake bread. My mother used the gold to gain passage for them on one of the ships taking refugees to Palestine.

Her brother Srul, who had been conscripted into the Russian Army during the war, was trapped in Russian-held territory and had to resettle in Russia. He later became a *refusenik*, the name given to a Soviet Jew who was refused permission to emigrate to Israel. He was jailed in a Siberia gulag and persecuted just for having asked to leave. In 1971 the Soviet Union lifted the ban on emigration but imposed an "education tax" for anyone who benefited from the Soviet Union's free higher education. My uncle had to retroactively pay for his tuition before emigrating. It was a considerable amount of money which my parents helped pay. Over 150,000 Soviet Jews emigrated to Israel during that period, including my uncle.

On my mother's side she lost her parents and her brother Itzhak. Also perished were Itzhak's wife Rifka and daughter Bracha. His other two daughters, Malka and Frida, survived and eventually moved to Israel. Malka later immigrated to America with her husband Gerhardt Basch and son Ilan.

16 LIBERATION AND THE AFTERMATH

When I asked my parents about what it was like to be liberated, I didn't anticipate the responses that I received. There were no celebrations, only relief that the nightmare was over. They made it clear that survival was still their overriding concern. The victims were in poor health without a home – no possessions, and not even the most basic of necessities. They didn't even know where their next meal would come from. During the worst of the COVID pandemic, people were asked to stay at home, wear masks and avoid socializing. Some strongly objected to the restrictions and loss of their freedom, while they were stuck at home watching Netflix and ordering food. I would shake my head at their outrage. I understood what deprivation was like. My parents and the other survivors were impoverished refugees, and no one wanted them.

For Holocaust survivors the war did not end with liberation. Despite the disappearance of the German guards and the arrival of Allied soldiers, there was no euphoria or celebrations. The soldiers told the survivors they were free to leave. And go where? They were weak, in poor health, and penniless. Thousands died after liberation. What they needed most was food and shelter. My father described how survivors traveled into a nearby town and walked away with food from shops. No one had any plans beyond making it through that day. Before the Displaced Persons camps were set up there were instances where Allied troops forced the inhabitants residing near the concentration camps to billet liberated inmates.

To care for and house survivors and those uprooted by the war, the Allies created Displaced Persons (DP) camps to provide temporary accommodations. Some lived in the camps for several years while trying to determine where and how to restart their lives. Conditions in the DP camps were bleak – many were set up in former concentration camps or German army camps – but the DPs also transformed the camps into active cultural and social centers. Approximately 250,000 Jews lived in the DP camps. Survivors were married and had babies in the camps. My cousin Regina and her husband Barek Eisenstein had their first child Sharon in the Bergen-Belsen DP camp. It wasn't until 1952 when the last DP camps were closed. In addition to those housed in DP camps, some survivors lived in accommodations in towns or cities across postwar Germany. My father avoided the DP camps, indicating they weren't much better than the concentration camps. He found accommodations first in Konstanz and later in Munich. In Romania, those liberated by the camps in ghettos in Transnistria found the locals equally hostile. After years of persecution, the survivors looked to emigrate and start a new life.

Most survivors no longer wanted to live in Europe because of ongoing antisemitism. Some looked for permission to emigrate to the United States and Canada, but both countries restricted immigration in the immediate postwar period. This was a continuation of a policy that excluded Jews who were attempting to escape Nazi persecution prior and during the war years. From 1933 to 1945 the US allowed in over 200,000 European Jewish refugees, while Canada accepted slightly over 5,000. Eventually, Canada accepted 40,000 Holocaust survivors, many with the help of Canadian Jewish organizations or family already living here. About 80,000 Jewish survivors immigrated to the United States.

Those who had survived the Holocaust had to come to terms with the loss of their family, home, friends, businesses, and all their personal possessions. For many there was nowhere and no one to return to. Some returned to their hometowns, only to be confronted by shocked and hostile former neighbors. Their homes and business were owned by non-Jews. Many of those tried to find out who had also survived. A child of Holocaust survivors described how her mother returned to Bedzin, and the Poles living in their home threatened to kill her. She escaped to the train station and immediately left town. Someone else's father ran into an armed group of Poles who were terrorizing returning Jews. Another Bedzin survivor reported that, when she asked the residents of her former home to allow her in to see it one last time, they refused.

The outbreak of pogroms following liberation was a warning that returning to Poland was fraught with danger. In 1945, a wave of anti-Jewish pogroms broke out across Poland, sparked by rumors that Jews were committing ritual murder. It was the age-old blood conspiracy theory that had made a comeback, which had Jews killing Christian children to use their blood to make matzah. The first such blood libel was in Chelm, in the spring of 1945. The Polish militia accused several Jews of drawing blood from a Christian boy. The next one took place in Rzeszow, in June 1945, when a body of a Polish girl was found in a building basement. A renter in the building was a shochet, and, not surprisingly, there were traces of blood in his apartment from the animals he slaughtered. The local militia claimed the girl's blood was drained from her body. As result, every Jew in town was arrested and subject to attacks. Assaults of Jews also took place in Opatow, Sanok, Lublin, Grojec, to mention but a few.

Jews were urged to move to bigger cities because they were considered more secure there. However, rumors of blood libels spread to cities as well. In June 1945, a Jewish woman was arrested in Krakow for allegedly attempting to kidnap and murder a Polish child. Rumors spread that the bodies of 13 Polish children had been uncovered. By August the rumored number had grown to 80. On August 11, 1945, a mob attacked the Kupa synagogue in Kazimierz quarter and set it on fire. The violence spread, leading to the death of a Holocaust survivor and five people injured.

As shocking as the Krakow pogrom was, the Kielce pogrom was a warning to Jews that it was far too dangerous to return to their previous homes. Kielce was home to 18,000 Jews before World War II. My friend Jack Kamrad's father, Harry, witnessed the pogrom. He was from Kielce and fled to Russia following the Nazi invasion of Poland, where he was conscripted into the Russian army. Following the end of the war he was transferred to the Polish army, but by the summer of 1946, he had left the army and returned to Kielce, as did a small number of survivors. On July 4, 1946, he witnessed a mob – including Polish police and Polish Army personnel – attack and kill over 40 Jewish survivors and injured dozens more. A few days earlier, an eight-year-old Polish boy had gone missing. When he reappeared two days later, he told his family he had been held by a man in a basement. As his father walked him to the police station to recount his story, the boy pointed at a man who was walking near a large building, which was owned by the Jewish Committee and was home to up to 180 displaced Jews. A mob attacked the building's occupants. Jewish men and women were stoned, robbed, beaten with rifles, stabbed with bayonets, and hurled into a nearby river. The attacks went on for hours. Harry Kamrad avoided being caught up in the violence because he was still in his Polish Army uniform.

Between the communist takeover and the pogroms, many Jewish survivors left Eastern Europe and made their way to Allied-held Europe. They had become stateless. The only family member who remained in Europe was my uncle Israel. The rest looked for elsewhere to re-establish their lives. They left for Israel, North America, and South America.

17 AN EYE FOR AN EYE

Shortly after the war my father and other survivors recognized a notorious former camp Kapo at a train station. A mob attacked and killed the man. This was not an isolated incident. In fact, Kapos were also subject to prosecution in the postwar years. During the trials in Gdansk, Poland of former Stutthof concentration camp guards in 1946 and 1947, five Kapos were sentenced to death. Israel prosecuted Kapos for several decades, beginning in the 1950s; one was even put to death. This created considerable debate and angst in Israel, as some did not agree with putting concentration camp survivors on trial.

Former Kapos were often pariahs within the Jewish community after the war. When I was quite young I was shopping with my father in Toronto's Jewish market when he spotted a former Kapo. I was shocked and frightened by how emotional Dad became. There was a long string of Yiddish curses from my red-faced father. The man was shaken but said nothing. He turned around and walked away while my father continued to scream at him. I was sure that had he been in possession of a weapon, he would have killed the man. I knew better than to have ever raised the confrontation with him.

Violence and revenge were a common occurrence during the period immediately following liberation. Jewish reprisals against former camp guards and officers continued for years, partly driven by the ease at which Nazis were able to return to civilian life. Some of these ex-SS guards would be strangled, and some were hanged, with the death made to look like a suicide. Several died in car accidents caused by mysterious mechanical failures. One senior Gestapo officer was waiting in a hospital bed for a minor operation when, somehow, kerosene got into his bloodstream and killed him.

Barek Eisenstein went to Katowice two weeks after his release from Auschwitz to join a group hunting down Nazis in Poland. The Provisional Polish government – which was formed by the Soviets – created an Office of State Security to assist in the arrest and prosecution of German war criminals hiding in Poland. The Russians encouraged the security service to recruit Holocaust survivors who were eager to seek revenge. As a member of the Katowice security office, Barek conducted raids on local Germans in hiding. During one such raid, he tossed grenades into a sewer, killing three SS men. The goal of the Office of State Security was the de-Nazification of Poland, which was not unlike Germany's efforts to remove all Jews from society. The security service recruits entered German homes and indiscriminately arrested German men, women, and children. Most of them were noncombatants and innocent civilians. Detainees were taken to cellars, prisons, and concentration camps, where they subsisted on starvation rations, contracted typhus, and were often tortured. Between 60,000 and 80,000 Germans living in Poland died in custody during this period. Jewish security officers were driven by their hate for the Nazis and the memory of their murdered family members.

I came across a remarkable story which illustrates how much survivors were consumed by revenge. Eliyahu Itzkovici was born to a Jewish family in Chisinau, Romania (now part of the Moldova Republic). During World War II, Eliyahu and his family were interned in Transnistria. As a young boy, he witnessed the murder of his parents and three brothers by a Romanian prison guard named Stanescu. Itzkovici survived the Holocaust and was liberated by Soviet forces in 1944, after which he took on the mission of hunting down Stanescu to avenge his family. He failed to find Stanescu, but located the man's son, who he stabbed to death with a butcher knife. In 1947 a Romanian court sentenced him to five years in a juvenile reformatory for the attack. In 1952, after being released, he was granted permission by the Romanian communist authorities to emigrate to Israel where he was drafted into the Israel Defense Forces and assigned to a Paratroopers Brigade. In Israel he learned that Stanescu had managed to escape into the French occupation zone of Germany and had enlisted into the French Foreign Legion. Itzkovici decided to continue the hunt for his family's killer. After completing his time in the Israel Defense Forces, he also enlisted into the Foreign Legion. Eventually he learned that Stanescu was serving with the 3rd Foreign Infantry Regiment stationed in French Indochina. Itzkovici tracked down Stanescu and shot him.

My father also participated in a reprisal. In 1946 while in Konstanz, he recognized the wife of a former SS officer walking on a street. He followed her home, broke into the house, and killed the woman and her child. When picked up by police, he brazenly admitted to the murders, indicating that the Nazis had killed his wife and daughter. The sympathetic police released him but ordered him to leave Konstanz. It seems that "an eye for an eye" was a justified defense in postwar Europe.

Revenge makes one temporarily feel better but does not eliminate or reduce the pain or trauma. I know how painful those losses were for my father, but these types of stories were told to me in "a matter of fact" manner. Maybe if I had undergone the same treatment, I would think differently. I never felt comfortable with the knowledge that my father was a killer.

18 NEW LIFE IN ISRAEL

The Arolsen Archives contain more than Nazi records. They also include records maintained by the Allied forces following the liberation of the camps. This allowed me to trace my father's movements in the early postwar years. There was a copy of an identity card issued by the French Army in 1946, indicating he was living in Konstanz, Germany. The card had "NON-DP" written across it which I presume was to indicate that he was not in a displaced persons camp. My father was on several lists maintained by the US Army of displaced person in Konstanz, confirming that he was living in Hotel Baden. I remember him bragging about how he lived in a hotel following liberation and now I had documentation confirming it. I have no idea how my father landed in a hotel while most survivors were consigned to a DP camp. My father's attitude coming out of the war was that, after losing everything, the world owed him. He expected payback and that mindset stuck with him over the rest of his life. In contrast, my mother was much more accepting. She felt what happened was horrible, but she held no grudges and wanted to move on.

Konstanz is a city on the German-Swiss border and was under French administration following the end of the war. Unlike many survivors, Dad chose not to go to a Displaced Persons camp or to return home. He considered the Displaced Persons camp as not much better than the concentration camps. Returning to Poland was not an option to which he was open. He claimed that the Poles were worse than the Nazis and that he would never return.

His anger towards the Poles was understandable. There was considerable antisemitism before the war, but there were also Poles who risked their own lives to protect Jews. A substantial number of Poles have been declared Righteous Among the Nations by the Yad Vashem, including the Prelate Mieczysław Zawadzki, who sheltered Bedzin Jews during a pogrom shortly after the Nazi invasion. After the fall of Poland, a Polish ambassador in Switzerland and his two principal aides obtained Paraguayan passports for Polish Jews through the Paraguayan consul in Bern, all without the knowledge of the government in Paraguay. There are no exact figures of the number of Jews who were saved in this manner, but it is said to be in the thousands.

The room that my father had at the Hotel Baden was paid for by the Allied forces. He even had a girlfriend, at least that's what he told family members. He quickly got involved in the black market. One of his early scams involved the concentration camp uniform. Allied authorities provided former camp inmates with civilian clothing to replace their camp uniforms. Dad would accept a set of clothing and then sell the items. He would show up in his camp uniform for another set and sell them too. He followed this routine several times before the authorities caught on and finally took away his camp uniform.

Dad would brag about his life of crime following his release from the concentration camps. Although I was skeptical at first, family members and friends corroborated some of what he said. Dad's career as a black marketeer would be best described as inept. In one case, he partnered with Barek Eisenstein, who married my cousin Regina after they met in Auschwitz. Dad was to buy black market diamonds, which they planned to sell for a profit. The diamonds turned out to be fake, which caused a rift in the family that lasted decades.

After a year in Konstanz he finally got in trouble with the authorities and had to leave. According the Arolsen Archives documents, Dad moved to Munich in early 1947 to join Uncle Israel. Dad's life of crime ended sometime in early 1948. He and his partner at the time had been smuggling watches from Switzerland and were finally apprehended by police. The two men jumped out of a second-floor window at the police station, and my father escaped on his motorcycle. His partner broke a leg and was apprehended. Dad decided to leave Germany and emigrate to Israel, which had just declared independence. On August 24, 1948, 577 Jews including my father left for Israel. They traveled by train to Marseille and then by boat to Haifa. The cost of the trip was paid by the US Army who were happy to find a country that would take displaced Jews.

My mother was the first of my parents to arrive in Palestine, as it was known before Israel was created. After several months in Suceava, my mother, Rachel, and David moved to Bucharest in late 1945. There they spent the next year-and-a-half arranging to make *aliya*, which is the Hebrew term for Diaspora Jews immigrating to Israel. They gained passage on a ship that was to illegally take them to Palestine. Much of the surviving Jewish population of Romania eventually moved to Israel following independence from Britain. Mom and Rachel left on one ship while David left on another ship later from a different port.

My mother and aunt boarded the *Max Nordau* on May 3, 1946, but their departure was delayed because the passengers had brought too many personal possessions which overloaded the boat. The ship finally left Constanta on May 7, with 1,754 passengers. It turned out to be the only ship to travel to Palestine from a Romanian port. The Romanian government decided to not let refugees leave from its ports following pressure from Great Britain, and Romanian Jews had to board ships in Bulgarian or Yugoslavian ports.

Illegal migration became the main form of Jewish entry into Palestine. Fourteen ships illegally transported about 24,000 Romanian Jews to Palestine during this period through an agreement between the Romanian government and Jewish leadership in Palestine in contravention of the British Mandate - but from other European ports. In fact, clandestine migration also took place during the war years. Not all made it.[1]

The *Max Nordeau* was apprehended by the British on May 13, and a British destroyer accompanied the ship to the port of Haifa. The passengers were sent to Atlit detainee camp outside Haifa. Uncle David's ship was also intercepted by the British navy, but he was sent to an internment camp in Cyprus.

In 2010 I visited Atlit. It had barbed-wire fencing, guard towers, and large barracks. Our tour guide described how new detainees were doused in DDT reminiscent to the delousing conducted by the SS at the concentration camps. I imagine that for many Holocaust survivors the experience would have triggered bad memories, yet Mom thought it was a

---

1. In 1941, 791 people died on the Sturma, which was sunk by a Russian submarine en route to Palestine.

pleasant place. They were released after five weeks of detention. Mom had no clue why, but I discovered the reason. To appease the Arab population, the British restricted the number of Jewish immigrants allowed into Palestine and prevented ships from landing. Those held in Atlit were eventually released and included in the quota of Jewish immigrants allowed into Palestine. Uncle David was not as fortunate. He wasn't released until after Israel's independence and at which time immigration was open to all Jews.

The ships carrying my mother and her siblings were just two of the 63 that left ports in the Mediterranean and attempted to evade the British blockade. All but five ships carrying illegal immigrants to Palestine were intercepted between 1945 and 1948, and about 26,000 Jews were interned in Cyprus.

Following their release, Mom and Rachel settled in Herzliya, just north of Tel Aviv. The town was named after Theodor Herzl, the founder of modern Zionism. Back then it was a rural community, mostly made up of Holocaust survivors with a population just under 5,000. Today it is an affluent suburb of Tel Aviv, known for its high-tech industry. For my family it was an exhilarating time to be in a country made up of fellow Jews.

Uncle David followed them to Herzliya following his release from Cyprus. Uncle Joshua, who had settled there in the 1930s after deserting from the Romanian army, found them a place to live and provided them with work at his farm, but Mom could not tolerate the heat working in the fields. They left Herzliya and moved to Afula, a village with about 2,300 inhabitants, located close to Galilee. She found a job at a hospital as an aide. This is where she met Dad.

Dad arrived in Israel after independence in September 1948 and was conscripted against his will into the army. Sometime after completing three months of basic training, he was assigned to a platoon. He convinced or bribed an officer to transfer him behind the lines. With his experience as a butcher, he was assigned to work in a kitchen preparing food for the troops.

Mom and Dad met shortly after my father arrived in Israel, sometime in late 1948. Dad first courted Aunt Rachel, perhaps because they were closer in age. However, they were hardly a good match. Rachel was too outspoken and independent; Dad was looking for someone subservient who would look after his needs. So he dropped Rachel and pursued my mother, who was 12 years younger than he was. He promised her that there would always be food on the table, which at the time was more important than love. He would bring her packages of meat that likely came from the army kitchen. This was not an insignificant gesture for someone like my mother who survived starvation. For survivors who had lost years of their life – not to mention family – under the Nazis, there was a great urgency to get married and start families. My parents were married on March 17, 1949.

I wouldn't describe my parents' relationship as based on love. Their marriage was a union that supported their survival and the need to move on with life. I don't recall ever observing an expression of love between them. It was as if finding love was a luxury that they could not afford. Perhaps it was typical of that time. Yet, their marriage survived for 59 years.

The animosity that developed between Dad and Aunt Rachel grew to the point where she refused to attend their wedding. I can only speculate that the acrimony was because both were too opinionated and stubborn to ever get along. Rachel stayed in Israel until 1955 and never married there. Aunt Mary had found her a man in New York, so she boarded an ocean liner in France and came to New York to marry Robert Kaplan. Robert was about 20 years older than Rachel and a widower. I uncovered the manifest filed with US Customs; my aunt had registered as Rachel Zloczower-Kaplan, although she had yet to meet Robert. So, it was clearly an arranged marriage. Rachel and Robert operated a fabric business in a bodega in Spanish Harlem for several decades. There was ongoing animosity between Dad and Rachel that continued to their graves. If her name was even raised in conversation, he would invariably make a face. When I was about eight years old, my mother had a severe gallbladder attack and was hospitalized to have it removed. She required several weeks of convalescing, and Rachel came from New York to look after me and my siblings. I'm sure there was considerable tension between her and Dad, but I was too young to be aware of it.

In 1979, several years after being widowed, Rachel moved from New York to Toronto. My brother and I rented a truck and drove down to move her. I distinctly remember the date because there was a major train derailment in Mississauga. As a result of the derailment, over 200,000 people were evacuated. We heard about the explosion in New York and had to come up with an alternative route to get around highway closures. The trip was longer than expected, but we finally made it home and my aunt lived out her years in Toronto. Mom was happy to have her around, but her relationship with Dad remained frosty. He would often say *ich ken nisht afile kuken oif ir* [I can't even look at her]. At times she could be irritating, but she was kind and supportive. My father was overly harsh when it came to her. We were also the only family she had. She lived to the age of 90 and passed away in December 2008.

My sister was born in Herzliya on December 27, 1949. My parents had to make do with what little they had. Similar to life in Israel, in Canada things weren't any easier. Mom used to tell us that for Tamara's first year, her crib was the drawer of a bedroom dresser.

My father claimed that he didn't like Israel's hot weather. I think there was more than the weather that motivated him to leave Israel. After all, Canada is not known for its fabulous weather. The joke in Canada is that there's only two seasons: two months of summer and ten months of bad weather. He would occasionally mention that he didn't survive the Nazis only to be killed by the Arabs. His survival instincts kicked in and he decided to leave for Canada in late 1952. His brother Moishe had already settled in Canada and sponsored my family.

At the conclusion of the war, Uncle Moishe had been transferred from Buchenwald to a Swedish hospital to recover from his injuries. His family made their way to a Displaced Persons camp in Bergen-Belsen, Germany. Eventually, they found him thanks to the Red Cross tracing services. With some difficulty, his wife Machela arranged passage to Sweden for herself and their daughter Jadzia. Jacob, Jadzia's partner, later joined them in Sweden where they got married. Regina who was now married to Barek Eisenstein and remained in Bergen-Belsen, Germany. In 1950 they all left to settle in Canada. In late 1952 my parents and sister left Israel, traveling back to Europe to arrange passage to Canada.

19 WALKING THE STREETS OF BEDZIN

I have always been curious about life in Poland before the war. If I asked questions, Dad would say nothing. If I pressed him, he would snap at me, "*laz mikh aleyn*" [leave me alone]. While some survivors were nostalgic for the hometown and spoke fondly of their early memories, my father was only bitter. I now realize that his silence was not an attempt to avoid the subject, but likely a defense mechanism against painful memories from the first half of his life. His silence and demeanor stifled my curiosity, and I wanted to avoid further traumatizing my parents. This is one of the ways that the parent-child roles can be reversed when the parents are survivors. The child will sometimes have to protect their parents from being hurt. I realize now that this was a mistake. I should have broken the silence and learned more.

I finally decided I needed to see Bedzin. Perhaps walking through the streets of the town would help me understand how my family lived (and died) and provide me some closure. The decision to visit Poland in August 2022 was not an easy one. I signed up for a group tour organized by a Facebook group that I belonged to known as the Bedzin-Sosnowiec-Zawiercie Area Research Society. The organizer, Jeff Cymbler, is a New York lawyer who has been tracing his own family's roots in the same region for several decades. Jeff has been to Poland dozens of times and has numerous contacts and resources. He is also the Bedzin town leader for JRI Poland, an important database that I used to research my family tree. Jeff is one of the most knowledgeable people on the history of the region and a wonderful resource. It made sense to join his tour group.

Mary Anne and Tamara joined me on this trip. I had mixed feelings about going because my father vowed never to return to Poland. He claimed the Poles treated him worse than the Germans. I consider this to be an exaggeration, but it also reflects the level of antisemitism that existed in Poland when he was growing up. Well before the German occupation Poles openly attacked Jews and boycotted Jewish businesses.

The Nazis were determined to wipe out any traces of Jews in Poland. But there I was, freely walking the streets of Poland, staying at fancy hotels, and relaxing at outdoor cafés. I don't think my father would have been unhappy about my trip. I think he would have been proud that I was there to defy the antisemites, whether real or imagined.

This was a difficult trip for everyone. There was one Holocaust survivor in the group. Tully Naftolin was 86 years old, just a child during the war and an uncle to Jeff Cymbler. On the first evening, we ate dinner in a private dining room is a Warsaw hotel. We each took turns to introduce ourselves. When we got around to Tully, he tried to explain how a Polish family had hidden him and his family for 22 months but couldn't finish. Such is the impact of the Holocaust almost 80 years later.

The trip had a several surprises. On the second day we visited Warsaw's POLIN Museum of the History of Polish Jews. While we were in the resource center Jeff Cymbler handed me a book of photographs of Bedzin Jews that had been sent to Auschwitz. I started flipping through the book and noticed a section about the Bedzin Jewish Orphanage. Aunt Sara had taught at the orphanage. As I looked at the photos taken at the orphanage I realized my aunt was in each photo. I was shocked by this discovery.

When I returned home I learned that Ann Weiss, the daughter of two Polish Holocaust survivors, was visiting Auschwitz in 1986 when she was shown a collection of about 2,400 photographs Jews had brought with them to Auschwitz, unaware of their fate. These photos included family portraits and candid shots, many belonged to Bedzin residents. Those on the transport were forced to surrender their belongings and suitcases, which included these photographs. The Germans required that all photographs be destroyed, to eliminate not only the victims, but their memories as well. Members of the Jewish underground in Auschwitz decided to stuff as many photos as they could into a suitcase which was then hidden. Those photos were in a storage room in Auschwitz for decades until they were shown to Ann by a museum official. She returned to Auschwitz to make copies of the photos and published a group of them in a book.

I realized that I must have had family members on that transport, perhaps Aunt Machela, who had been sent to Auschwitz with her children following the liquidation of the Bedzin Ghetto. The timelines seemed to make sense. Three days later I would visit 17 Sienkiewicza Street, the building which had housed the orphanage. It was a large four-story building that has served several purposes over the years. The children in the orphanage were sent to Auschwitz in June 1942, shortly before the major deportation in the summer. Afterwards, it was used by the German authorities as the gathering place for Jews who were to be deported to Auschwitz or other camps until they could be loaded onto trains. Following the August 1942 Aktion, Jews to be deported – including members of my family – were held in the vacated orphanage. The building, which was later adopted for a children's hospital, has now been out of use for many years; and considering its large size it might never be used again.

It was an emotional day walking the streets of Bedzin. You have an image in your mind of what you expect to find. I was eager to see the town but, as we arrived, I experienced some apprehension. Would the town look as it did in the 1930s and 1940s or had it undergone revitalization? Would I find the buildings where my family lived? In fact, there are some modern buildings and new highways, but the original apartment blocks, the train station, schools, factories, and laneways were still there. It looked liked a grimy industrial town you might find in the US rust belt. The major difference is that there were no Jews left; no Jews walking the streets, no Jews in the open market, and no Jewish-owned businesses. On Malachowskiego Street was the Jerusalem Café, a Jewish-themed restaurant without any Jewish patrons. So much history took place here, but it left me with a void.

My day started at the records office in the town hall in search of the original documents used to register my dad's marriage to Estera, as well as the births of Laja and Jenta. Jeff Cymbler had arranged for me to be taken to the municipal offices by Adam Szydlowski, a member of the town's council. Because Dad had never mentioned Jenta, there had always been doubt in my mind about whether he was aware of her birth. Maybe he was sent away to the camps before she was born? I had asked to also see the marriage registration for my dad's sister Jentla, who was married around the same time as my father. Since I was not a direct descendant I was not allowed to see that due Polish privacy laws. It made no sense to me because she had no direct descendants and I was the closest living relative. The clerk retrieved a large binder for the year 1941. I carefully looked over entry number 322 (Dad's marriage registration), 360 (Laja's birth registration), and 361 (Jenta's birth registration). The documents revealed that Estera's mother,

Laja Cypa Kupka, had died when Estera was 12. I realized that my father and Estera had named their first daughter, Laja, in her honor. The clerk allowed me to photograph the three entries. At the bottom of the entries was my father's signature. I literally had to catch my breath. There was no doubt that at some point he had held Jenta in his arms in 1941. The same pain that made him bury those memories brought me to tears.

Looking for evidence of the Bedzin Ghetto so many decades later was a challenge. It was hard to imagine that 20,000 people could be crammed into a few blocks of the old Jewish quarters near the old market square. In fact, someone had to show me where the old market square had been. At the time, the Great Synagogue was considered the heart and soul of the Jewish community. A memorial granite obelisk stands at the site on the main road, in the shadow of the medieval castle of King Casmir the Great. This was one of several memorials to the former Jewish residents in the town. The monument was in the shape of a *tefillin*, a small black leather box containing scrolls of parchment inscribed with verses from the Torah and worn by Jewish men during weekday morning prayers. It was a strange place to stop as the memorial was at a busy intersection with a lot of traffic, and the monument itself was small and barely noticeable. While we stood around the granite stone, we each lit a memorial candle. The Great Synagogue and the buildings that stood adjacent to it were destroyed and have never been rebuilt. It's now a grass-covered open space, which only added to the bleakness of the area.

I went up the road behind where the synagogue had been. It was here that panicked worshippers ran up the road to take refuge in a church, the Parish Church of the Holy Trinity while being fired at by German soldiers. It was such a short route, but it must have felt forever on that night.

Later in the morning we were brought to two restored shtiebels. The first stop was the Mizrachi Shul, a prayer house established at the start of the 20th century in the basement of a house owned by Jakub Chil Winer, a merchant. It was a private prayer house and the only one in Bedzin to survive the Holocaust. It served as the basement for the residents of the building until 2004, when a Holocaust survivor identified it as the place where his family prayed. It took five years to restore. It was a small shul with beautifully painted walls and ceiling with incredible details depicting holy sites like Rachel's tomb, the 12 tribes of Israel, and the Hebrew months.

Our next stop was the Cukerman prayer house at 24 Kollataja Street. The shtiebel was on the second floor of a run-down tenement building that for years was used as an apartment for Polish families. During the war the Nazis used it as a warehouse, which was common practice. The prayer house was established in the 19th century for the Cukermans, a wealthy Jewish family. We were met there by Karolina and Piotr Jakowenko, founders of the Cukerman's Gate Foundation, who explained the history of the prayer house and the restoration which they took responsibility for. It was uplifting to hear how committed they were to educating Bedzin residents about the once flourishing Jewish community. Miraculously, the stunning paintings that decorated the walls were never destroyed. They had been painted over with latex paint, which was removed without damaging the artwork underneath.

We had lunch in the Foundation's offices, and I ducked out a little early to walk down the street to the site of the old Jewish market. I'm sure my father wouldn't have recognized it. There was an open square in red interlocking bricks just off Kollataja Street. On one side had been the wet market where my father and his brothers operated their poultry shops. It wasn't very large, so it must have been crowded with shoppers prior to the war. That day no one was there so I left and walked down Modrzejowska Street looking for apartments rented by my dad and Uncle Moise. I believe I did see it, but I can't be sure; the street numbering had changed since the end of the war. It could have been a rundown tenement building with a cement stucco exterior painted gray.

Later, we walked through the streets of the former Kamionko Ghetto, passing by the house where Rutka Laskier wrote her diary from January 19, 1943, to April 24, 1943. The diary remained hidden under stairs until retrieved by her Polish friend Stanislawa Sapinska. Not far away, at 24 Rutka Laskier Street, was a building that was used by the ghetto resistance. Bunkers had been created in the basement and under a nearby barn. The occupants of the bunker fought back against the Germans when the ghetto was being liquidated in August 1943. After several days of resistance, they ran out of ammunition and were killed. The importance of the uprising was more symbolic than strategic. It was one of a small number of acts of armed resistance taken by Jews held in a ghetto outside Warsaw.

We also visited the Plac Bohaterow Getta Bedzinskiego [Heroes of the Bedzin Ghetto Square], in the central part of Kamionka, where in 2005 a monument was erected to commemorate the sad ending of the history of Bedzin Jews. It was a simple, yet striking message. The monument consists of the structure that represents a cattle car and a piece of railway track symbolically leading to Auschwitz. We paused to light memorial candles.

Earlier in the day, we made a stop at the Copernicus School, which at one time was 40 percent Jewish. After an English teacher, Iona Bonos, showed us around she joined us for the rest of the morning. While we walked through the town center, I mentioned to her that I wanted to see my grandparents' apartment block, if it was still around. I showed her the address and she said it was just a few hundred meters from where we were standing. She offered to take me there. We walked down Malachowskiego Street, which was the main street of what once was the Bedzin's Jewish Quarters. Many of the prewar apartment buildings still exist and are occupied. I stopped in front of 38 Malachowskiego, the building where my grandparents had lived. They occupied a first-floor unit. The first level of the building was painted in a mix of pink, gray, beige, and orange. The rest of the building had the color of weathered cement stucco. Stamped into the cement was "1934", the year the apartment was built. In the center of the building was an archway that led into a courtyard. I walked through the archway to look around. As I stepped into the courtyard, shivers went up and down my spine. I felt like I had been there before. I wondered if my imagination was playing tricks on me. I took out my phone and flipped through the photos until I reached the one that I had been carrying with me for the past six months – that same photo of my grandmother, my aunts Jentla and Mariem, Estera, Laja, and Jenta, sitting in a grass-covered courtyard. I had always hoped that if I showed it around to people in town, that someone would know where it had been taken. Although 80 years had passed, the windows in the buildings surrounding the courtyard looked the same as those in front of me. The grass in the courtyard had been replaced by pavement. I realized that I was standing on the same spot that the photo had been taken. I never expected this moment to occur, and I was overcome with emotions as my eyes welled up.

The trip to Poland was also intended to include visiting places of significance to the Oksenhendler family. I arranged for us to be driven to the region of Poland where my ancestors had originated from. Our first stop was Wislica, where my father and previous generations of Oksenhendlers had been born. There was nothing to see in Wislica. Any evidence of my ancestors was gone. The village was once home to 2,500 residents with about 1,500 Jews. Now there were only 500 villagers, and none of those were Jewish. I would have loved to have visited the home where my father was raised, but I couldn't find any information on the location, assuming it still existed. Where a synagogue once stood, there was a bleak communist-era apartment building. The Jewish cemetery had been destroyed – partly during the Holocaust when gravestones were used by the Nazis for road construction, and partly afterward by residents using the stones for various purposes. We found the cemetery overgrown and barely accessible. I discovered a few gravestone fragments sticking out of the ground. In the village's main square, there was a memorial to the victims of the Nazi occupation. The memorial had a crucifix and made no mention of the village's Jewish residents who were the primary victims of the Nazis. This could be why my father had such a negative opinion of the Poles. I just wanted to walk the streets and be surrounded by the spirits of my ancestors. It was my only opportunity to feel them. I knew I would never return.

We next drove to Pinczow – where my grandmother was born – which was 25 minutes away. We first stopped at an old Renaissance-era synagogue, one of the oldest in Poland. It had been badly damaged during the Holocaust, which led to its disuse. The structure was restored in the 1970s as a museum. While speaking to Renata, a woman who worked for the museum, I mentioned the surnames of family members that had lived in Pinczow: Oksenhendler, Tragerman, and Sledzik. She mentioned that a Polish woman in the town was a Sledzik (Estera's family name) but assured me that this woman refused to discuss her past. I indicated that I would still be interested in reaching out to the woman. Renata said she would pass on my contact information. Several weeks later, a woman named Marta (a pseudonym) contacted me. It was not the woman living in Pinczow, but her daughter who lives in Spain. Marta confirmed that her family was Catholic, but the family secret was that they had Jewish ancestors. Her mother refused to talk about it because Pinczow is a small town and antisemitism still exists. Marta knew very little about her Jewish past but had discussed it with her mother after I had reached out to them. She told me that her grandmother was born Gitla Sledzik, and her great-grandparents were Moszek Wolf Sledzik and Laja Cypa Kupka. I immediately recognized the names of her great-grandparents because they were on my dad's marriage registration. Moszek and Laja were Estera's parents. It turned out that Gitla was Estera's younger sister. She had married a Pole in 1934 and changed her name to Genowefa Stanek. The family disowned her after she had converted to Catholicism, but it likely saved her life. During the war, Gitla was hidden by her husband when the Germans were deporting the Jews of Pinczow to the Trebinka death camp in October 1942.

Based on this information, Marta was a grandniece of Estera. Marta asked what other family members were still alive (her grandmother had seven siblings). I informed her that, as far as I could determine, Marta, her mother, her aunt, and her two sisters were likely the only living descendants of the Sledzik family. She was upset by the news but glad to have some closure.

Like many Poles in Marta's situation, she is curious about her Jewish ancestry.

Krakow was one of the more interesting legs of our trip. Krakow was where events covered in Steven Spielberg's film *Schindler's List* took place. Much of the film was shot in Krakow, and shortly after its release, tourists would show up to see the "Schindler's sites." Tour companies and guides leaped into action, taking tourists to see the Schindler's factory, the Krakow Ghetto, and Placzow concentration camp. In addition, you could visit locations around the city where the movie was filmed. It was rather underwhelming. The factory, where a few of the factory scenes were filmed, was turned into a museum. Other than memorial plaques, essentially nothing is left of the Ghetto or concentration camp.

The transformation that had taken place in the Kazimierz district of Krakow was rather fascinating. What had once been the old Jewish quarter had become a trendy tourist site. The abandoned Jewish establishments had received facelifts, while trendy bars and Jewish-themed restaurants had been opened. The remaining Kazimierz synagogues were now renovated, although only one synagogue is occasionally open for religious services, because there no longer are enough Jews in Krakow. The other synagogues are used as museums, bars, or bookstores. For young Poles, Jewish culture was now hip. This was not my father's Poland. There were no shtetls or Jewish markets, and very few shtiebels. I felt no different than visiting Roman relics in other parts of Europe.

On day 11 we visited Auschwitz-Birkenau. I was filled with dread and the bus trip to the complex was in silence. I couldn't stop thinking about my family that came here before me. It was likely 80 years to the day that they were transported in cattle cars that were so crowded that they could only stand, whereas I was making the trip in a comfortable bus with the air conditioning blasting out cool air. In 1942 the 30-kilometer train ride from Bedzin to Birkenau took about four hours. The people crammed into the cars were likely filled with terror because by the summer of 1942 it was common knowledge what was going on in the concentration camp.

In 2019, the year prior to the coronavirus pandemic, 2.3 million people visited Auschwitz-Birkenau. It's now a museum and a significant tourist attraction. The museum claims there is no entrance fee, but they stipulate that groups must have a licensed guide (you bring your own or the museum can provide one) and that comes at a cost. The Poles have done a wonderful job at preserving Auschwitz, but it also bothered me that it has been commercialized and has become a little too sanitized.

Our Auschwitz tour guide took us through former blocks that had been converted to exhibits that sent shivers down my spine. In Block 4, a glass case was filled with human hair. There were hundreds of kilograms of hair that hadn't made it to Germany for the purpose of stuffing mattresses or manufacturing textiles, socks, and carpets. It's conceivable that some of these carpets still exist and are in use in Germany.

Another glass display contained a cannister of Zyklon B. In Block 5 we saw a mound of artificial limbs and crutches and another display was filled with pots and pans. There were piles of suitcases with the former owners' names scrawled on them, and a huge collection of spectacles. Viewing the collection of children's shoes was like a punch in the gut. Every pair represented an innocent child that was murdered. Children just like Laja and Jenta. I will never be able to understand how anyone can murder children. Can people have this much hate? This was not the act of a few individuals but of an entire nation.

The bleakest part of the tour was Birkenau. Just walking towards the entrance was chilling. It was a hot and humid August day and there was no shade or water. The grounds were immense, spanning 350 acres. Enough of the camp was intact that you could envision how this place was once a sophisticated killing center. The railway tracks running into the complex still existed. It's all still there – the barbwire fences, the row after row of blocks where the prisoners lived, the guard towers, blown-up remains of the gas chambers and crematorium, even a solitary cattle car. We followed the railway tracks from the main gates into the center of Birkenau. We stopped where the tracks ended, and where the train platform once stood next to Crematorium III. Each train transport carried between 2,000 and 3,000 people, which matched the capacity of the crematoria. Crematorium III once had five groups of ovens with three doors on each oven although none of these details were visible.

We lit candles next to the crematorium and a rabbi in our group led us through Kaddish [the Mourner's Prayer]. In the distance, I strained to see where Bunker #2 had once stood. It was the second gas chamber in Auschwitz. Also known as the "Little White House" that had been set up in a farmhouse, expropriated from a Polish farmer from the village of Brzezinka before permanent gas chambers were constructed.

This is where my family was taken shortly after arrival. When transports arrived at night, the victims were hauled in trucks to the killing site. The new arrivals were accompanied by a car with the emblem of the Red Cross and guarded by SS. That car carried the poison gas and an SS doctor with medicines plus an oxygen bottle for use in an emergency, such as the accidental poisoning of SS men taking part in the gassing.

The victims were told that before taking up residence in the camp they had to go to the bath and undergo delousing. They had to remember the spot where they left their effects. They were told to undress, either in the barracks or outside behind the hedges. I visualized Estera carrying the two little girls into a gas chamber. What kind of a world does nothing to stop this type of madness?

The weight of being in the presence of such evil made it hard to breathe. Despite the heat, I found myself shivering. Tears ran down my cheeks. I realized that I was standing where once such evil existed. I recited out loud the names of my dead relatives. Birkenau was their gravesite. For some of my family members, it was the first time that Kaddish was ever being recited on their behalf. Eighty years late, but better late than never.

20　TRAUMA AND MEMORY

Until I began seeking historical documents for this memoir, I had no idea that my half-sister, Jenta, ever existed. Why would Dad have kept the existence of Jenta hidden? It made no sense. This is how I finally understood the role that trauma played here. He had subconsciously buried the memory. As a Sonderkommando he would have understood that babies were gassed and burned in a crematorium. Babies that were the same age as Laja and Jenta. How painful that must have been, not knowing the fate of his own children? I have no background in psychology, but I do know that when faced with traumatic stress, the brain can suppress memories. There is no other explanation that makes sense.

Trauma also would explain why my father never talked about the family members who perished in Auschwitz. I knew he had five siblings but that was it. I didn't know their names or ages of his two murdered sisters. It was only through my research for this memoir that I was able to uncover information about the family. I discovered that his oldest sister, Jentla, was married to Mordka Lejb Sledzik, who was the brother of my father's first wife. They were married, together with my father and Estera. Dozens of cousins also perished. My paternal grandfather had nine siblings and my grandmother had seven. Most of the siblings and their children did not survive. My mother's family was not impacted to the same degree but there were still many victims. These were horrific losses to endure. I feel that sense of loss despite never having met any of these relatives.

The impact of trauma experienced during the war manifested itself differently for my mother. She fixated on food her entire life. She too had certain memories lapses. She was open to discussing her experiences during the war, but I noticed that there were numerous details she couldn't recall. I eventually concluded that she also had suppressed memories. In my mother's 1995 interview by the Shoah Foundation, she was asked a series of questions to help her recall her story. There were many blanks in her recount of the war years. The interviewer gently tried to prompt her, but Mom claimed her mind was blank.

My extended family members were equally traumatized by their experience. They suffered from depression, paranoia, and nightmares. They tried to bury their grief and painful memories and live normal lives with varying success. Perhaps that is why I enjoyed the company of my mother's sister who had left Europe before the war. There wasn't nearly as much emotional and psychological baggage.

Trauma was obviously not unique to my family. It showed up in other survivor families; although, when I was younger, I didn't discuss with friends how messed up our parents were. I first became aware that there were common patterns of behavior exhibited by survivor families in 1979, with the release of Helen Epstein's book *Children of the Holocaust*. She was born in Prague in 1947 and grew up in New York. Epstein set out to find a group of people who, like her, were influenced by a history that they never lived. She reached out to second-generation survivors in North America, South America, Europe, and Israel. She interviewed hundreds of men and women, each struggling to cope with their legacy. To say that her book resonated with me would be an understatement. I discovered that my family's experience was not unusual. But at the same time, the experiences could be radically different. For example, some survivors raised their children as Christians, and never told them of their Jewish past to protect them from any possible antisemitism. It's ironic that all I have been able to find of what remains of Estera Sledzik's family are Catholics.

Epstein's book initiated an interest in children of survivors for sharing their experiences growing up. The first conference was held in New York in 1979 attended by mostly Americans. In 1981 there was the World Gathering of Jewish Holocaust Survivors in Israel. Second-generation survivors were one of the topics discussed. Several years later there was the First International Conference of Children of Holocaust Survivors. I watched all these events from a safe distance. I was interested but not ready to share my own experiences. It took many years before I became active in Toronto's community of children of survivors.

Most traumatic experiences happen in response to things like physical abuse, emotional abuse, neglect, addiction, and witnessing dysfunctional relationships. When we have a trauma response we go into fight (attack), flight (run away), freeze (play dead), or fawn (appease or people please). For Holocaust survivors, appeasement was a very common response because the others would often be lethal. This is our nervous system responding to threats. These responses help us mobilize or immobilize – to survive the threat. Trauma becomes stored within the body in the way we breathe, make eye contact, our posture, our coping mechanisms, and our habitual emotional responses. Therefore, understanding and processing past trauma is important: because we tend to relive it in cycles (also known as generational trauma).

Dr. William G. Niederland was a New York psychoanalyst whose observations of former concentration camp inmates led him to formulate "survivor syndrome" as a distinct condition in 1961. It was derived from his interactions with 2,000 patients who survived the camps, as well as survivors of other traumas, including natural disasters and accidents. In his study, Dr. Niederland observed symptoms, including insomnia, nightmares, personality changes, chronic depressive states, disturbances of memory, anxiety, and psychosomatic ailments. He used these studies and his work with Vietnam veterans to embody the concept of post-traumatic stress disorder (PTSD) as a recognized diagnosis.

Depression was a common thread throughout the survivor community, including our family. This form of depression was different. Those affected were typically not provided an opportunity to bury or mourn for loved ones. Instead, they carried around repressed mourning, that often came to the surface when family and friends passed away during the postwar years. In other situations, I saw a total lack of emotions, because this was an important survival skill when you are experiencing death and depravity every day.

In the late 1970s, studies on Vietnam veterans who had difficulty returning to civilian life led to the recognition of post-traumatic stress disorder (PTSD). Many Holocaust survivors suffered from PTSD, but there was no diagnosis or treatment for the disorder following the war. Holocaust survivors suppressed their most painful memories, but certain events would serve as triggers and bring them to the surface. My family's decision to move my mother into a retirement home had a traumatic effect on my father. At first, he refused to join her, but after several months of living on his own, he relented. He was miserable and refused to participate in any of the programs. Within a few weeks he refused to eat. What we didn't grasp at the time was that the move had triggered wartime trauma. He was experiencing a flood of memories that he had mostly suppressed for much of his life.

I once sat down to itemize what I learned or inherited from my parents. It turned out to be an interesting list. My father normalized sarcasm to the point where I assumed that's just how you spoke to people. One time, my brother made a "family sarcasm jar" as a deterrent. Whoever said something sarcastic was expected to deposit a quarter into the jar. Within a day I pulled out because I realized this was only going to lead to financial ruin.

People often ask me how I came by my sense of humor. It wasn't only trauma that was passed down in my family. There was also humor which was a response to the trauma – in particular self-deprecating humor. Trauma and guilt are shadows. Sometimes, they are easier to recognize than the light that casts them. From my limited experience, humor might be one of the lights we received from our family.

Maybe the right question to ask is what is the origin of Jewish humor? It appears to be a distinctive cultural phenomenon that bloomed in the shtetls in 19th-century Eastern Europe. Jewish humor didn't thrive only in marketplaces, synagogues, and homes, but was part of the culture and folk tradition. Jewish writers such as Sholem Aleichem and I.L. Peretz, mined the bittersweet grumbling of the Jewish ethos and produced lasting classics of Jewish humor, which in turn fed the comic banter of Jewish daily exchange.

It's all about coping: Jews were miserable, and laughter kept them going. Living in those shtetls, Jews were always a minority, surrounded by gentiles. Even when not actually under threat from their neighbors, that fear was always around. Their jokes were most often self-deprecating. They targeted themselves, their dire circumstances, or their religion.

If my father was stopped by a friend and asked, *"vos machstu?"* [how are you? or how are you making out?], he would often respond with, *"ich macht nisht visen"* [I make like I don't know]. This was a Yiddish play on words. But it also reflected his attitude in life – don't get involved or bring attention to yourself. I can see where he was coming from. In the camps, bringing attention to yourself could lead to a negative outcome. In 1965, when

Holocaust survivors showed up at a Toronto park to protest a rally by neo-Nazis, my father was not among them. Over time, I exhibited the same trait. I was reluctant to be in the spotlight and not good at selling myself or my accomplishments. I was also predisposed to burying my emotions. Yet, it made it easy to come up with self-deprecating humor

Yiddish curses and put-downs always brought a smirk to my face. These included *"kholere oif dir"* [cholera on you]; *"fardrey zikh dany kop"* [drive yourself crazy], which literally translate as "twist your head around"; and my favorite *"du zolst vaxn vi a tsibele mit deyn kop in der erd aun deyn fis in der hoich"* [may you grow like an onion with your head in the ground and your feet in the air], which needs no literal translation. My dad's humor included playing on words, double entendre, and lots of sarcasm. I didn't just hear it from my dad, but his contemporaries as well. They brought this humor to North America, but as that generation died off and the next generations assimilated, that style of humor died out. There are no shtetls left.

My father believed that he survived the camps because he was a hard worker and provided utility to his captors. That work ethic was passed on to us. I became driven at work to avoid a negative outcome instead of trying to gain advancement. I was motivated by a fear of failing and losing my job. Even after being recognized on multiple occasions for my work achievements, that irrational fear remained.

My parents were not risk takers. In fact, they were extremely risk adverse. There were times when this was a source of frustration and conflict. From my perspective, living in fear wasn't really living. But I can also understand their perspective; they could no longer trust the system because it failed them miserably. I share some of that mistrust. Police and military personnel have always been a source of anxiety for me. They are supposed to protect me but how can I be sure that the opposite won't happen? When the protectors become oppressors, there is no one to turn to. I never really found that comfort zone.

Trust was always an issue for my father. On two occasions, Dad went into business with a friend. Those partnerships did not end well because he trusted no one, not even his own family. His trust issues used to bother me, but I now understand that this was at least partly attributed to his wartime experience. How much of his behavior could be attributed to trauma? We can never know but I'm convinced it was a factor.

Because he was averse to any level of risk, it made running a business and investing money difficult. Late in life, much of his savings were in Treasury bills and Canada Savings Bonds, which tells you all you need to know about his risk profile. He owned commercial properties in Toronto during the 1960s but did not hold onto them for long. In one case, a tenant was late making a single payment, which stressed him out so much that he ended up selling the property for a loss. By the 1960s we were no longer considered poor because my parents worked hard and long hours, which always compensated for all other shortcomings.

My parents had no understanding of the reasons for antisemitism. It was just something that was always out there. They tend to be guarded around non-Jews. I couldn't really blame them. In fact, I've always reacted poorly to antisemitism. It made me angry, but it also made me afraid. I have always wondered whether what happened to my family in Europe could happen in Canada. When I encountered an antisemitic slur, I typically said nothing and moved on. I told myself not to ruffle feathers. Throughout my life, I wanted badly to fit in and be like everyone else, partly denying who I really was. At times I tried to hide my Jewishness, which was impossible to do. You would have to be from Mars to not realize I was Jewish. I now realize that what I had been doing was detrimental to me, and only emboldened the racists who harassed me. My approach has changed significantly in recent years.

Why did I become this way? Beginning as a child and into my adult life, I had recurring nightmares in which police would come to our door at night to take us away This was in addition to my dreams about being in a gas chamber. Throughout my life I subconsciously believed the Holocaust was going to happen again. I still do. Every act of antisemitism reinforced that belief. Being called derogatory names. That happened in prewar Europe. I've been told several hateful things such as, "too bad Hitler didn't kill you all." I know there are people who would be happy to see us dead. Graffiti painted on synagogues or on buildings housing Jewish businesses and organizations, that also happened before the war. The Boycott, Divestment, Sanctions (BDS) movement aimed at boycotting businesses that operate in Israel, boycotting Israeli academics, and pressuring artists to refuse to appear in Israel? The Nazis led boycotts of Jewish businesses, academics, and artists. I have no intention of debating Middle East politics, although I support the state of Israel. I raise these things because they are a source of anxiety for me.

I also learned to bury unpleasant memories. Both my parents were capable of this, but my father experienced this phenomenon to a greater extent. Memory reacts to trauma closing off access to painful events. As I struggled to remember events from my childhood while working on this book, those memories reached my consciousness along with buried trauma. In 2023 I decided to seek out therapy. That process released even more trauma. Over time, I became acquainted with the concept of intergenerational trauma.

When the war between Israel and Hamas broke out in October 2023, it was a difficult time for me. The images of the October 7 attack reminded me of the pogrom that took place in my mother's village on August 2, 1940. I experienced nightly dreams, thoughts of pending disaster, and hypersensitivity to antisemitism. I was not alone. A month after the attack, I attended an event for children of survivors. There were group sessions with facilitators to share personal experiences. Everyone was experiencing the same. One thing that struck me was that every participant indicated that it was a good thing their parents were no longer living. That is because we knew that our parents' generation would be suffering far more trauma than we could possibly experience.

Even before Helen Epstein's book *Children of the Holocaust*, I was reading about the Holocaust and Nazi Germany in my teens, including *The Rise and Fall of the Third Reich* by William Shier, *Hitler: A Study in Tyranny* by Alan Bullock, *Inside the Third Reich* by Albert Spiers, and *The Diary of a Young Girl* by Anne Frank. But the experience for me was not what one would expect when reading history books. Those books produced considerable anxiety. For me, it was about trying to understand how something like the Holocaust could even happen. I needed to understand the context for the persecution and murder of my family.

Not only were Holocaust survivors the subject of various studies but so were their children. In 1966, Canadian psychiatrist Dr. Vivian M. Rakoff and his colleagues recorded high rates of psychological distress among children of Holocaust survivors, coining the concept of "generational trauma." Since then, researchers have continued to study anxiety, depression and PTSD in Holocaust survivors and their children.

A 1988 study published in *The Canadian Journal of Psychiatry* found that grandchildren of Holocaust survivors were overrepresented by about 300 in psychiatric care referrals.[1] Since then, Holocaust survivors and their

---

1. "Grandchildren of Survivors: Can Negative Effects of Prolonged Exposure to Excessive Stress be Observed Two Generations Later?" John J. Sigal, Ph.D., Vincenzo F. Dinicola, M.D.,

children have been a widely studied group, but in theory any type of extreme, prolonged stress could have adverse psychological effects on children (referred to as just 2G) and/or grandchildren (3G), resulting in clinical anxiety, depression, and post-traumatic stress disorder (PTSD). Some patterns have emerged, including a sensitivity to antisemitism and a general concern about their safety. It is common to see first-generation survivors pass on depression and anxiety, displayed often in parenting, instilling a higher sensitivity in subsequent generations. Studies suggest that 2G are more likely to experience psychiatric conditions than the general population, and that they tend to be overachievers and to possess a finely honed sense of humor. It's been noted that the pandemic increased many people's levels of anxiety, and that would include survivors and their children.

During the first month of the pandemic lockdown in 2020, I heard from my brother daily as he coped with high levels of anxiety. He complained of nightmares. I also experienced an increase in anxiety, and, in response, I buried myself in writing projects to distract me from a sense of doom that weighed heavily on me.

But on the plus side, survivors also exhibit considerable resilience and a natural ability to cope with disaster. That resilience has allowed survivors to pick up their shattered lives and re-establish themselves in new places, with new cultures and languages, raising their families, and passing down stories of survival. But for 2Gs it is different. Resilience means discovering their own parenting style, their own approach to adversity, and determining how to tell their parents' stories. For 3Gs it is also different. Often their parents serve as a buffer to their grandparents' trauma and resulting lifestyles; 3Gs are less burdened and can better navigate relationships.

Intergenerational trauma doesn't just affect individuals. It can impact a whole group or community, too. In this case, the definition of intergenerational trauma refers to the collective complex traumas inflicted on people who share a specific identity or affiliation. That might mean their ethnicity, nationality, or religion. This isn't the exclusive domain of Holocaust survivors. The transatlantic slave trade and colonialism of indigenous people have shown that intergenerational trauma can devastate whole communities across decades and even centuries. That's because intergenerational trauma involves what happened in the past, but also

---

and Michael Buonvino, B.A. View, *The Canadian Journal of Psychiatry*, April 1988, Volume 33, Issue 3

what's happening in the present and what will continue to happen in the future. A legacy of trauma forms in which a community continues to experience distress over generations, despite never having experienced the original trauma.

A 2015 study suggested that children of Holocaust survivors may have been marked "epigenetically," chemically coating their chromosomes to create a kind of biological memory of their parents' experience. As a result, some suffer from a general vulnerability to stress, while others are more resilient. Previous research assumed that transmission was caused by environmental factors, such as the parenting behaviors. New research, however, indicates that these transgenerational effects may also have been genetically transmitted. Integrating both hereditary and environmental factors, epigenetics adds a new comprehensive psychobiological dimension to the explanation of transgenerational transmission of trauma.

21 WHO NAMES A CHILD WILLIE HANDLER?

I have had to endure years of ridicule because of my name. Who names a child Willie Handler unless they are planning a porn career for that kid? When I changed schools in grade seven, I used Bill as my given name, but I never felt comfortable with it. By the end of the school year I hated it. In grade eight I was in a new school and went back to Willie. On social media I've joked about it being a pen name or pseudonym for so long, that many people aren't quite sure what my real name is. I was named after my maternal grandfather Wolf. We share the same Yiddish name (Velvel) and Hebrew name (Zev). My parents were new Canadians and barely knew any English. Someone told my mother that Willie was the English version of Wolf. Willie Oksenhendler wouldn't have been so bad, but my parents were also told to change our surname to Handler. To this day I get strange looks when I'm asked for my name. The follow-up question is typically what name is on my birth certificate.

I sometimes wonder what my life would have been like if my parents had remained in Israel. I know I wouldn't have been named Willie. It's not that I don't like life in Canada. It's an exceptional place to live, with a stable society and political systems, protection of human rights, universal health care, and a high standard of living. But it gets so cold here. By midwinter, I sometimes question what I'm doing in this frigid country. But if the war had not occurred, or if my dad hadn't moved to Israel, then my parents would never have met.

Uncle Moishe, who was already in Canada, had agreed to sponsor my family. Once the proper documents were finalized, they packed up to cross the Atlantic. My parents didn't have enough money to make the trip, and only got as far as Paris, where they stayed for three months. They found an apartment, and my dad found some work. The family joke was that I am a Parisian because I was conceived while Mom was in Paris. They left Paris for England and boarded the *Scythia,* a Cunard line ship, in Southampton on March 20, 1953.

At the time, the *Scythia* was the longest serving ocean liner in the Cunard fleet, having first sailed in 1921. She became a troop carrier during World War II, and in 1948 *Scythia* was given to the International Refugee Organisation to take refugees from Europe to Canada. In 1950 she became a passenger ship again, sailing from Britain to Canada and later to New York. I never found my parents listed in a shop's manifold, but I uncovered my dad's immigration card that indicated they arrived in Halifax on the *Scythia* on March 29, 1953.

Traveling in steerage was not a pleasant experience. Dad was sick the entire trip. He often declared that it had been the worst experience of his life. That would usually have me rolling my eyes, considering his war time experience. The trip was just over seven days as the ocean liners in that era were much faster than today's cruise liners. The *Scythia* docked at Pier 21, which served as a passenger terminal for trans-Atlantic passenger liners from 1928 until 1971. Pier 21 was the primary point of entry for nearly one million immigrants and refugees from Europe and elsewhere. It was an immigration official at Pier 21 who suggested that my parents anglicize our surname from Oksenhendler to Handler. Uncle Moishe shortened his surname to Hendler when he arrived in 1950. When Uncle Israel's family arrived in the 1960s, they continued to use Oksenhendler as their surname. As a result, all three brothers had different surnames.

We were *greeners* [greenhorns]: new Jewish-Canadians without money, social status, or a safety net. My impression was that you were not fully accepted by Jews who were born in Canada. We called them *gayle,* which literally means "the yellow ones." Ironically, their families had all been greeners at some point. Unlike today, immigrants were looked down on. It was demoralizing to have Canadian-born Jews turn a nose up at you because your parents were born in Europe. By 1960, survivor families made up 20 percent of Canadian-Jewish households. As a result, we were minorities not just in Canada but within the Canadian and Toronto Jewish community.

After clearing immigration, my family boarded a train to Ontario and got off at Galt, about 100 kilometers west of Toronto. The evening of March 30 was the start of Passover and all they had to eat was a *vursht* [salami] that Dad had brought with them. That was their *seder* [ritual service and dinner for the first two nights of Passover] meal that evening. Uncle Moishe continued the family link to the poultry business and had purchased a chicken farm in Galt (now Cambridge) in southwest Ontario. Living at the farm was my aunt and uncle, my cousin Jadzia, and her family. Now there were three more. I'm not sure how long this arrangement was to have lasted, but there was considerable tension almost from the start. They looked down at my mother because she was Romanian, and they were all Polish. You would think that people who had barely survived genocide would be sensitive to their own prejudice. My experience over the years has been that this wasn't always the case.

Dad soon realized it was time to move on. He reached out to Norman Ciminsky from his hometown of Bedzin who at the time was living in Toronto. Norman and his wife Sylvia owned a house on Oxford Street in the Kensington Market district. My parents rented their second-floor until they could afford to buy their own house. This was the typical immigrant experience in the New World: find cheap accommodations until you can afford your own place.

During their first year in Toronto, Dad held down three jobs and earned about $45 a week. His experience as a butcher got him a job at Toronto Packing Company, one of the chicken processing businesses owned by the Ungerman family. It was located on Spadina Road just north of St. Andrews Street in Kensington Market. The Ungermans were immigrants, arriving in Canada from Poland just before the start of World War I. They opened a kosher poultry store in Kensington Market before getting into chicken processing. The Ungermans often hired newly arrived Canadians – including Holocaust survivors – during the wave of immigration that followed World War II. One of their sons, Irving Ungerman, was also a well-known boxing promoter who managed and represented Canadian boxing champions George Chuvalo and Clyde Gray.

Dad slaughtered chickens, working 12-hour days from Monday to Friday, and half-days on Saturday. Overnight on Friday, he baked bagels for Lottman's Bakery in Kensington Market. He slept much of Sunday and was then driven by truck to Guelph to pick up live chickens from farms in the area for the Toronto Packing Company. For several months my mother also worked at Toronto Packing, plucking chickens. She had no one to leave my three-year-old sister with, so she brought her to work. This didn't go on for long because I was born in September. She showed up at Mount Sinai Hospital early on the morning of September 20. She knew almost no English at the time and had difficulty communicating to the hospital staff the reason she was there. She did not come through the emergency room, and the staff assumed she had come for one of the hospital's clinics. Initially, they told her that it was Sunday and that the clinics were closed, suggesting that she would return on Monday. After a Yiddish-speaking doctor showed up, she was finally able to get them to understand that she was in labor; I was born later that day. I came into this world weighing just four pounds and nine ounces and spent the next six weeks in an incubator.

22 MY EARLIEST MEMORIES

When I think about it, it was quite remarkable that just over a year after coming to Canada with nothing more than the clothes on their back, my parents scraped together enough money to purchase a house. We moved into a three-story, semi-detached house on Bathurst Street in The Annex district of downtown Toronto. The area got its name in the 19th century because it was one of the first districts north of Toronto to be added to the city. It was a beautiful residential neighborhood with tree-lined streets and Victorian and Edwardian houses.

The purchase price was just over $3,000, which is equivalent to under $40,000 today based on inflation. The current value of that house is over $1.5 million, which suggests that Toronto real estate was a good place to put your money. Shortly after we moved, my brother Irv was born on April 6, 1955.

The house was built in the 1920s and used to have a coal-burning furnace, because the chute for the coal delivery was still at the side of the house. When we moved in the house's heating had been converted to an oil-burning furnace with hot water radiators. There was an oil tank in the basement, which a company would come around to fill periodically. The basement had a dirt floor and a heavy odor from the heating oil.

One of the reasons we could afford the house was that we only used the first floor while the second and third floors were rented. The first floor had three rooms: a kitchen, dining room (which was a bedroom for me and my siblings) and living room (which was my parents' bedroom). The living room had a pull-out sofa and a 16-inch black-and-white Westinghouse television which served as our only entertainment. Like most people at the time, we had an antenna on our roof, which allowed us to pick up three Buffalo stations in addition to the local ones. For the first few years, there was a Greek family living on the second floor. The only bathroom in the house was on the second floor, so everyone in the house had to share that one bathroom. As a small child, I remember being washed in the kitchen sink when the tub was unavailable. The Greek family had people come and go. It seems we were housing members of their extended family. For a time, my parents also rented the third floor. By the time Tamara reached age ten, she moved up to the third floor when it was deemed to be no longer appropriate to be sharing a room with two brothers.

Today, I would find these living conditions to be intolerable. But as a child you accepted it. Being reminded how bad it was in Europe reinforced the notion that we were doing well. Although on the rare occasion, when we visited relatives in the new suburbs, I couldn't help but notice the contrasting lifestyles with their modern bungalows on big, landscaped lots.

The Annex was a mixed neighborhood that included Jewish and other ethnic immigrants. Next door was an older woman, Mrs. Holloway, who did alterations from her home. Living with her was her granddaughter Brenda, who was close to my age. We had almost no toys or games in our house, but Brenda did, so I ended up playing there a lot. Our home only had the bare necessities, and toys did not fall into that category.

My parents spoke only Yiddish at home. At the age of four, I refused to speak Yiddish and insisted on using English. That is why I understand Yiddish but struggle to speak it. Picking up English was a slow and painful process for them. My mom eventually learned to read and write some English. My father was illiterate other than reading Hebrew, which all Jewish children were taught. I was always embarrassed by their broken English and heavy accents. My dad would mix up words, like pronouncing "anniversary" as "universary," for example. Today, I'm ashamed that I was embarrassed by their struggle to learn a new language.

Despite my reluctance to speak Yiddish as a child, it has always had a special meaning for me. I miss hearing it. In 2016, there was a touring theater company that came to Toronto and did a stage version of Arthur Miller's *Death of a Salesman* in Yiddish. It was an unusual play to stage in Yiddish because, although Miller was Jewish, the characters in his play are not. Watching the production and hearing that familiar language brought me to tears.

One of my earliest memories was being in the hospital at the age of four. I had a wandering eye. It's not unusual for one or both eyes of a newborns to wander. They typically straighten out after a few months. Mine did not. My mother dragged me to several doctors, and it was decided that I would get corrective surgery. I distinctively remember my hospital stay and that it was a frightening experience. The surgery was a partial success. I was left with a lazy eye and went years with a patch over my good eye. It was torture walking around not seeing well. I would pull off a corner of the patch so that I could see. It failed to improve my vision and to this day I still have that lazy eye and rely on my good eye to see. As I grew up, I was very protective of my eye, particularly when playing sports.

I wasn't the only one in the family with this problem. Tamara also had a wandering eye but by the time my mother took her to a specialist, it was too late to correct it. My nephew Josh also has the same problem, and he too was tormented with patches over his good eye.

I was a sensitive and shy child. I didn't easily make friends at school and would break into tears if criticized by a teacher. I was picked on at school because of my mother's fashion tastes, my name, and for the frequent patch I wore over my right eye. I was taunted with things like "Silly Willie with the two by four haircut." It didn't help that I did grades three and four in the same year. Our school had an acceleration program which I was put into. Tamara and Irv also accelerated. I was already one of the smallest in my class. Now I would be that much farther behind my peers physically. It only contributed to my feeling of not fitting in and created a social gap throughout my years at school.

The sidewalk on our street is where we played, mostly without adult supervision. No one was concerned about having their children playing outside, even on a main roadway like Bathurst Street. Irv and I are 19 months apart in age. When we were young, we played together much of the time. As we grew older we slowly grew apart, developing different friends, interests, and temperaments. However, during those years living on Bathurst Street, we hung out together. I remember one time when we were playing baseball in a neighbor's backyard. I was batting and Irv was catching, except he caught the bat in the head instead of the ball. He ended up with a lump on his head the size of the ball and a concussion. I was not the favorite child that day.

While many survivor families moved into the new suburban development called Bathurst Manor, we did not. For the first ten years of my life, we remained in Toronto's Annex district.

Growing up, I didn't have an extended family that I was close to because my mom didn't have family locally, and my dad's family didn't get along. Each family unit kept to themselves, which I never fully understood because there were so few of us. It was ironic that we came from these large families that went through a great deal together. Now we were alone.

The few times the extended Handler family got together, my dad and his brothers would invariably argue and curse at each other – *mashuguna* [crazy person], *mumzer* [bastard] or *nar* [fool]. It never made sense to me that these surviving family members would always be at each others' throats. Dad and Uncle Israel spent much of the war together in the same camps where they constantly looked after each other. If they were able to get some extra food, they would share it. If one of them were to be receive a beating, the other would care for the wounds as best as they could. Despite their shared experiences, I would not have described their relationship as close. We typically only saw family at weddings, funerals, and bar mitzvahs. When it came to the holidays, we celebrated alone.

In 1961, the St. Alban's Boys Club (since renamed the St. Alban's Boys and Girls Club) opened on Palmerston Avenue in Vermont Square Park. It was a wonderful facility for my family because the programs were free. I enjoyed hanging out there, playing sports and board games, and swimming after school. I joined their boxing club and was undefeated, but that fall I had to quit to attend afternoon Hebrew school.

We wanted to wear clothes that Canadian kids wore, which rarely happened. Clothes were bought at Kensington Market or Honest Ed's, a landmark discount store at the corner of Bloor and Bathurst Streets until it closed in 2016 for redevelopment. Honest Ed's was the place every generation of new immigrants shopped. They had "door crasher" specials that produced long lines of shoppers, waiting for the store to open – things like a tube of toothpaste at 25 cents or two pairs of work socks for 75 cents. I would stand in those lines with my mom. Clothes were worn until they were no longer salvageable. Mom sewed patches over the holes that would appear in the knees of our pants. I hated those patches. She also knitted us ugly zip-up cardigan sweaters with caribous that are now considered kitschy. I had nothing but contempt for those sweaters. When we grew out of them, she would unravel the sweater and use more yarn to make a larger size. Our nicest clothes were gifts from our New York relatives.

Every Saturday afternoon, I went with my siblings to the movies. There were two second-run movie theaters on Bloor Street, just over a kilometer from our house. The Midtown Theater was opened in 1941. It had an interesting history. During the 1950s attendance at the Midtown slowly dwindled and switched to showing horror films. In 1970s it screened censored adult films which contained scenes that today are often shown on regular television programs during primetime hours. Today it is the only theater in North America specializing in documentary films, and it is the home of the annual Hot Docs Canadian International Documentary Festival. The other movie house, the Alhambra Theater opened in 1920 as a venue for movies and vaudeville. It also showed porn films in the 1970s until it was demolished sometime in the 1980s. Those theaters were beautiful but couldn't compete with the multiple screen venues.

Each Saturday we would walk down to Bloor Street with a bag of popcorn that was popped at home, and we decided which of the two theaters had the better films. They both provided a double feature for 25 cents. Mom would provide us with just enough money to cover admission. One Saturday we showed up and the price for children had increased to 35 cents. Since we only had 75 cents, we had to return home. The first time I saw a first-run film was *Babes in Toyland,* which was released by Disney in 1961. We traveled by streetcar and bus to Eglinton Avenue in midtown Toronto to see it in the Nortown Theater. I was in awe of this ultramodern theater, with its plush upholstered seats that were spaced wide apart.

Another regular outing for us was to walk to the Wychwood branch of the Toronto Public Library. The library branch opened in 1916 and was housed in a brick building with polished hardwood floors. Wychwood library is on Bathurst Street, just over a kilometer north of where we lived. I was reading at age four, although I'm not sure how I started reading, since my parents barely spoke English and my sister was just eight. I was an avid reader, and every three weeks I would check out six books, which was the maximum number you could take home.

Tamara was enrolled in Palmerston Public School in 1954. I followed her in 1958, with Irv entering in 1960. At age eight, I started attending *cheder* [a school where you were taught Hebrew and religion] after elementary school. I was there from 4 p.m. to 6 p.m., Monday to Thursday, with another two hours on Sunday mornings. This killed all extracurricular activity until I had my bar mitzvah at age 13. The cheder was part of Eitz Chaim School, which had a satellite branch on Burnside Avenue several blocks north of where we lived. We walked there and back each day. It was a one-room school taught by Rabbi Orbach, a Holocaust survivor with no discernible teaching skills. He was a firm believer of corporal punishment and walked up and down the classroom with a yardstick. If anyone was out of line, he would shout *"Gib der hant"* [Give me your hand] and dispense a violent whack on the palm. He was a nasty man, and he once broke his yardstick on the head of a student. After several years, the Burnside location was closed, and we were transferred to the main Eitz Chaim campus in the Toronto suburb of North York, where we were placed in separate classrooms based on age. We now had to take public transit, and our day was further extended. It meant we had dinner when we got home at about 6:30 p.m. and then did our homework.

In the early years, our household was a mix of Orthodox Judaism and more lax observance. Mom came from an extremely observant home and kept all the Jewish dietary laws. Passover was important. Food purchased had a rabbinical sticker certifying that it contained no prohibited food. It was a lot of work for an eight-day holiday. On the major holidays of Rosh Hashanah and Yom Kippur, we didn't turn on lights or watch television. My father was not as observant. He was a traditionalist in his religious observance, although I never got a sense of how observant he was prior to the war. Dad never allowed religion to get in the way of making a living. He worked and drove on the Sabbath, and we went to the movies every Saturday. Yet, we were sent to an Orthodox Hebrew school. Like every Jewish family, our religious observance became a matter of choice. People decide on how they will practice religion and create their own rationale.

Our family never belonged to a shul. That was a financial commitment that Dad was never prepared to make. You can attend services all year long for nothing except for Rosh Hashanah and Yom Kippur. The concept of supporting Jewish institutions did not interest him. On the High Holy Days, non-members could attend services at a synagogue by purchasing tickets. So, that's what Dad would do. He would look for the most inexpensive tickets and that's where we would attend services.

While we lived downtown, we attended services at the First Narayever Synagogue on Brunswick Avenue in The Annex. It remains an active congregation and is one of a small number of synagogues that remained downtown following the Jewish migration up the Bathurst Street corridor in the 1950s and 1960s. It was originally an Orthodox shul, which means that the congregation followed strict interpretation of Jewish laws and prayers and resisted any modifications or accommodations to reflect the modern world. In the 1980s, the Narayever evolved into an egalitarian congregation, with men and women participating equally in a traditional service.

When we attended services, it still had a *mechitza* [a barrier or curtain] at the back of the pews to separate the worshippers by gender, because Orthodox men and women never sit together in public. The services were not child-friendly and entirely in Hebrew. Irv and I sat with Dad and Tamara sat with Mom in the back. It didn't take long before we became bored and hung out outside with other kids. At the time, the neighborhood had tall mature oak trees, and in fall the ground was covered with acorns. Before long, we would be firing acorns at one another until an adult came outside and scolded us.

After we moved north, Dad decided on a storefront shul below a billiard parlor. The women were crammed near the entrance behind a wooden divider, which served as a mechitza. Here, the entire service was also in Hebrew except for the sermon and announcements, which were in Yiddish. It was the 1960s, but I felt like I was in a Polish shtiebel except this one was on Wilson Avenue in the Toronto suburb of North York.

23 GUILT TRIPS

The thing that most stood out to me about growing up with my parents was how we always lived under the shadow of the Holocaust. There was constant tension at home when my father was there. He easily lost his temper and could become abusive. So much of his behavior and moods I attribute to his experience. He needed to be in control of his life and would acquiesce to no one.

We did little together as a family. When I was out having fun, I would inevitably feel guilty about it. It wasn't necessarily intentional, but that's how I felt. That's why I would always joke that our family vacations were guilt trips.

In the early years there were some family outings. My father would drive us to a park for a picnic on a Sunday during the summer. Those daytrips ended when my dad purchased businesses that were open seven days a week. We might take the ferry to Centre Island in the Toronto harbor. Sometimes we would pack up the Pontiac and head out of the city. There was a conservation park on Heart Lake in Brampton that we occasionally visited. On rare occasions we would go to Jackson's Point on Lake Simcoe. It was a narrow strip of parkland on the southern end of the lake where a lot of survivor families would go to escape the summer heat. We often went to a privately owned park and beach on Musselman's Lake in the Oak Ridges Moraine in York Region. Because it was a private park, there was paid admission. My parents paid for themselves and then snuck us in.

The one thing that stood out for me growing up was that I always felt different from the other kids in the neighborhood and at school, including the Jewish kids. There were some survivor families, but not many that I was aware of. I never discussed my parents' experiences with friends, not even with those kids that had similar backgrounds. Many of the stories in this book have never been shared with people outside the family. Perhaps if we would have lived in a largely survivor neighborhood like the Bathurst Manor suburb, my experience would have been different. My parents spoke with heavy accents while most of the other parents didn't. My friends' parents had nice clothes and good jobs – they were accountants, lawyers, or pharmacists. They did things that we never did, like go on vacations. My parents didn't play bridge or golf and didn't belong to a private club. Many kids had large families and even grandparents. When they talked about their grandparents, it put me in a funk. I wanted all that attention and the experience of being spoiled. My grandparents were part of me but that wasn't enough.

"*S'iz gut in Amerike*" [it's good to be in America] was a phrase that I often heard at home. Sometimes it was meant to reflect how well things turned out for our family in Canada, but the comment had a double meaning. It could also be a dig, intended to induce guilt. You have it easy here while I suffered in Europe. It might slip out as I was heading out to a party or after buying a new car. Maybe it wasn't supposed to be a shot, but it sure felt like it. Guilt was the go-to method to get us to do what my parents wanted. It often worked but the problem with guilt is that you can't bottle it up. It lingered in the air like the stale smell of cigarette smoke.

Not only did my parents dish out guilt but they had to deal with their own. My parents, like many Holocaust survivors, experienced feelings of guilt – not because they did something wrong but because they lived. There was nothing my father could have done to save his parents, wife, and children, and that weighed heavily on him. The guilt of surviving is passed on to future generations.

There were expectations placed on me because such opportunities were not available to my parents. As much as I resisted attempts to feel guilty, it was always present. My guilt was driven by the knowledge of how difficult things had been for my parents. Was I to blame? Of course not, but I couldn't help from trying to shield them from further pain. So, I never asked questions even though there were things I wanted to know. You avoided subjects that would trigger the tears. I had to learn to be independent because my parents were so wrapped up in trying to survive the postwar years. Except now it wasn't physical survival, but instead emotional survival.

24 EVIL FACELESS BUREAUCRAT

Our otherwise dull lives were shattered in 1960 with the capture of Adolf Eichmann and his subsequent trial the following year. Eichmann, under the direction of Reinhard Heydrich, was responsible for the implementation of the "Final Solution" – the murder of all European Jews. He was assigned to facilitate and manage the logistics involved in the mass deportation of Jews from ghettos to extermination camps in Nazi-occupied Europe.

Eichmann became renowned for his ruthless dedication to the systematic slaughter of Europe's Jews, and his extreme efficiency in carrying out his mission. When Heinrich Himmler, ordered him to send all Hungarian Jews to Auschwitz-Birkenau as quickly as possible, Eichmann allegedly described the assignment as "a fantastic opportunity." He had a new rail spur at the death camp built which saved time on the Birkenau end of the line. The trains could now stop within a couple of hundred meters of the gas chambers. I walked alongside that set of tracks built for Eichmann when I visited Birkenau. I shuddered at the thought of these evil people looking for ways to kill more efficiently.

After Germany's defeat in 1945, Eichmann was captured by US forces, but escaped from a detention camp and traveled across Germany under false identities. He moved to Argentina with help from groups that were sympathetic to the Nazis. He was eventually tracked down by the Mossad, Israel's intelligence agency, which sent a team of agents to kidnap Eichmann and smuggle him out of Argentina to stand on trial in Israel. He was found guilty of 15 charges and hung in 1962.

His capture and trial have since been the subject of numerous films and books, but I remember watching the trial. It was a chilling experience even at my young age. The trial lasted 56 days, over a four-month period, and was front page news around the world. Unlike the Nuremberg Trials, which relied extensively on written documents, the prosecution in the Eichmann Trial used over 100 Holocaust survivors as witnesses, although many had never met Eichmann. Their objective was not just to put the defendants on trial, but also the Holocaust itself. It was an educational opportunity that is sorely needed today. The media coverage, particularly the coverage of the emotional testimony from survivors, resulted in an increased interest in the Holocaust. The Israelis arranged for the trial to be taped, and we huddled around our television much like we did several years later when the Apollo 11 astronauts landed on the moon.

I was not yet eight years old. The trial moved my Holocaust experience beyond just my own family. I don't remember if there was any discussion of what was going on within our family beyond the curses of my parents directed at the perpetrator of these crimes, but the trial had an impression on me. It put a face to the evil atrocities described by my parents. What did that evil look like? Just like a faceless bureaucrat you would come across when renewing a driver's license. That is what was most unnerving about it. He didn't look like a monster at all.

25 BLOOD MONEY

In 1952, the first Israeli Prime Minister David Ben-Gurion, along with the Conference on Jewish Material Claims Against Germany (often referred to as the Claims Conference), reached an agreement with the Federal Republic of Germany to compensate Holocaust survivors for losses during World War II. You wouldn't think that was a controversial decision within the Jewish community at the time. But, in fact, it was.

Some survivors saw it as blood money and wanted no part of it. They felt that being compensated for dead family members was vile and no amount of money would be adequate compensation. Some refused to apply. Even those that decided to collect reparation payments had mixed feelings. The same debate took place in Israel. The *Knesset* [Israeli parliament] narrowly passed a resolution to enter direct negotiations with West Germany. Outside the Knesset, thousands of Israelis protested and rioted the decision, leading the police to use tear gas to disperse the crowds. Over the years, controversy continued to plague the Claims Conference with accusations of fraud, corruption, and mismanagement.

In my family there was no such debate. My parents had lost not just family members, but also their property, livelihoods, and years off their lives. Dad believed he was entitled to compensation for the years he was forced into slave labor. Reparation payments would never compensate him for these losses. How could it? It didn't replace his loved ones. It didn't heal the physical and mental injuries. It certainly didn't ease the pain, resentment, and anger. My parents came out of the war with nothing, and money would improve our family's standard of living. Those cheques helped rebuild my parents' lives. This was the reason that the decision was made by the Israeli government to seek compensation.

The application process was complicated and created a group of lawyers and doctors that specialized in reparation claims. To support his claim, Dad provided a notarized letter from a lawyer, providing details of his Holocaust experience such as injuries, property losses, and details of loss of liberty and other hardships. The medical examinations were limited to physical problems and didn't consider psychiatric or neurological conditions. Some survivors who had undergone beatings came out of the Holocaust with undiagnosed head injuries.

I was too young to remember my father applying for reparation payments, but I received copies of his supporting documentation from the Arolsen Archives. There was a document sent to the International Tracing Service (the predecessor to the Arolsen Archives) requesting a Certificate of Incarceration listing the camps he was held in during the war. The Certificate of Incarceration was issued on March 6, 1951. International Tracing Service noted that his camp records were incomplete because many documents no longer existed. It was through this document that I could confirm in which camps my father was imprisoned, because it was not something discussed at home. He resented the requirement to present himself annually at the German Consulate in Toronto with a life certificate to continue to qualify for restitution. Having to face German bureaucrats would put him in a foul mood for several days.

Initially, my mother wasn't eligible for compensation because Transnistria wasn't considered a concentration camp when the original agreement was reached. My mother felt hurt by this omission as did many Romanian survivors. She always felt her Holocaust experience was trivialized by the Jewish community. It wasn't until the late 1990s, over 50 years after liberation, that Transnistria was recognized as a Nazi ghetto and my mom became eligible for a lump sum payment. It bothered her a lot that her wartime experience was not initially recognized – it only exacerbated her trauma. For a time, even I didn't fully comprehend how horrific it had been for her.

Israel had an interest in the original negotiations because they wanted to be compensated for the cost of absorbing and rehabilitating the Holocaust survivors in Israel. An important aspect of the negotiations was that West Germany acknowledge that they had committed "unspeakable crimes," and that restitution did not absolve them of responsibility for these acts. The agreement paid a portion of the payments to Israel and the Claims Conference received the portion that was to go to Holocaust survivors.

As a result of ongoing negotiations with Germany, eligibility for reparation continued to expand. For example, in 1953 agreements were reached with several German companies that used Jews as forced laborers including Krupp, Siemens-Halske, Dynamit Nobel, Daimler-Benz, and Volkswagen. Eventually, the Swiss banks negotiated funding for victims behind the Iron Curtain, and for victims of medical experiments. My mom and the Transnistria survivors were one of the last groups to be compensated.

I was a grown adult when my mother asked me to complete her application for reparation payments 50 years after the end of the war. Although there were no gas chambers in Transnistria, there were certainly executions, death marches, humiliation, typhus outbreaks, starvation, beatings, and terror. People were dumped in a barren region with no amenities. The goal was no different – the total annihilation of Romanian Jews. It's a senseless exercise to determine who suffered more.

26 THE SHTETL MARKET IN TORONTO

For the first eight years of my life, my world was tied to Kensington Market. The market was comprised of several streets running off Spadina Avenue south of College Street, including Baldwin Street, Augusta Avenue, Nassau Street, Oxford Street, and Bellevue Avenue. Our first Toronto home was in Kensington Market. My father's first job was in Kensington Market.

Dad's work experience in Poland was in the poultry trade so it was easiest for him to find employment in similar businesses after arriving in Canada. He eventually moved on from his job at the Toronto Packing Company and found another job in Kensington Market. He sold poultry and eggs for a widow, Mrs. Seiden. The business was not much different than the one he had in Poland before the war.

I visited Seiden Poultry store several times and it was identical to the other chicken stores in the market. There were wooden crates out front crammed with chickens. I felt bad for the birds. Conditions for the birds were deplorable, and they looked so distressed. The shop had a table outside loaded with eggs. Inside, there was a counter and refrigerated display with eggs and butchered chicken, and a large butcher block where chickens were cut up. The floor was covered with sawdust, which absorbed any spilt blood and helped contain odors.

I thought it odd that some customers bought live chickens. They carried home the chicken wrapped in newspaper with the head sticking out like a bundle of flowers. Most would pick out a chicken and have it slaughtered while they waited. If the customer wanted a kosher chicken, Dad would take the bird two doors down to a laneway where a shochet operated a ritual slaughtering business. He was always dressed in a smock splattered with blood. There would often be water mixed with blood streaming down the laneway into a sewer after he hosed down his premises.

If the customer didn't require a kosher chicken, Dad would kill the bird himself by slitting its throat. To save money, some customers took the chicken home to pluck the feathers and clean the bird themselves. Most preferred it to be prepared at the store. The freshly killed bird would be submerged in warm water to make it easier to pluck. A torch was used to singe left-over pinfeathers and hair. The store would smell of burnt flesh after a bird was defeathered. Finally, the feet and head were cut off, and the bird was gutted.

It was quite the show for a six-year-old. This is one of the reasons that I developed a dislike for chicken. And of course, when I got home, my mother would serve chicken for dinner.

Much of our food and other necessities came from Kensington Market. My dad would bring home a 50-pound sack of potatoes or a basket of peaches from the market, which were stored in the basement. When I needed rubber boots or a raincoat for camp, I was taken to one of the market vendors. You could buy just about anything at the market. With my dad involved, that also included a large dose of haggling, insults, and curses – all in Yiddish. Many family members started off in the Market. For example, my cousin Jadzia and her husband Jacob Eisenstein operated a grocery story on Spadina Avenue. Regina and Barek Eisenstein had a kosher butcher shop on Kensington Avenue.

To this day, when I walk through the streets, I drift back to the sights and sounds of the charming and bustling Jewish market of old. Wooden cages crammed with squawking chickens, tanks of live fish, barrels of pickles and salted herring, the smell of fresh baked breads and cakes, venders barking out their wares: "Cherries, cherries, cherries!" and "A nickel a pickle!" It was noisy, smelly, and dirty. But I always felt comfortable there.

It had the atmosphere of a shtetl market, but in a modern North American city. It was what we would call *haimisha* [homey]. My comfort level had nothing to do with prewar Europe. I was born in Toronto. It was the people. They were like us. People spoke Yiddish, and their broken English didn't feel out of place.

The market housed numerous landmark businesses. There was Shopsy's Deli on Spadina. Hyman's Bookstore was also on Spadina, where we bought all our religious articles, including my first *tallit* [a prayer shawl], as well as material to prepare for my bar mitzvah. On College Street there was Koffler Drug Store, which was opened by Murray Koffler's father. Murray went on to establish the Shoppers Drug Mart chain in 1962. Also on College was Health Bread Bakery, where the *shtitzlach* [blueberry bun] was introduced to Toronto Jews. Local folklore has it that Annie Kaplansky brought these Ashkenazi treats to Toronto from her hometown of Rakow, Poland, when she moved here in 1913. She sold them in her bakery Health Bread Bakery which she opened in 1928, and they became an instant hit. When I visited Poland in August 2022, I tried the Polish version which were similar but less sweet.

By 1960, there were over 100 Jewish restaurants in the area. The last surviving restaurant was The Bagel on College Street, and it closed in 2006. It was affectionately known as "The Dirty Bagel," a name what was well deserved. The crowded restaurant looked like it couldn't possibly pass a health inspection. My favorite place was Lottman's Bakery on Baldwin. My special treat was when my mom would buy a fresh chocolate-glazed donut that would melt in your mouth. Mrs. Lottman was always behind the counter, and before ringing up your purchase, would always ask: "Something else please?"

From my perspective, Baldwin Street had always been the heart of the market. When you walked down Baldwin, you could see retractable awnings outside most businesses, prominently displaying their names and providing some protection from the elements. Merchants wore long white aprons stained from the blood of chickens and fish, or rotted fruit. Vendors started out selling goods from pushcarts a generation or two earlier. Likely because they were tired of pushing their carts, they built permanent stalls in front of their homes. This was the origin of the "Jewish Market." The next stage was the conversion of the ground floor of their homes into stores, although they continued to display their wares on the sidewalk, as is done to this day. Many transactions took place outdoors on the sidewalk, even in winter, with merchandise in wood bushel baskets.

I was most familiar with Baldwin Street because my father worked on the street for many years. It was entertaining to witness the interaction between him and a *landsman* [a compatriot]. One might ask the other, *"Vos macht a Yid?"* which is equivalent to being asked, "How are you?" but literally translates as "How is a Jew?" The other would then answer with: *"S'ken alemol azyn beser"* [It could always be better] or *"S'ken alemol zayn erger"* [It could always be worse], or my dad's personal favorite, *"Ich macht nisht visen"* [I don't know]. This was language brought to Canada from the European shtetls.

But not all the sights and smells were pleasant. What attracted many shoppers was the wet market with numerous fish and poultry stores carrying live fowl and fish. I was occasionally taken to a fish store owned by Barek Weizenberg, who was from Dad's hometown of Bedzin. They carried mostly fresh fish that was displayed on ice, but they also had tanks containing live fish. This is where my dad bought his live carp which would reside overnight in our bathtub. For those that preferred their fish killed and gutted, Barek would bash it in the head with a bowling pin before preparing it.

The stench in the summer months was horrible. The live chickens in wooden crates that lined the sidewalk in front of the poultry stores were loud and equally foul-smelling. On occasion, a chicken would break free and scurry around the sidewalk. Throughout the 1970s, animal rights activists and the Toronto Humane Society – which the city had hired to be its animal control agency – pressured lawmakers to ban the sale and slaughter of poultry and rabbits in the market. In June 1983, the animal control bylaw was passed, and live chickens, rabbits and fish disappeared from Kensington.

By this time, Kensington was no longer a Jewish market. The north Toronto suburb of Bathurst Manor attracted many Jewish home buyers, and most of them were Holocaust survivors looking for larger properties and lower prices than what could be found in the downtown core. The migration north impacted Kensington Market. Although Jews still operated businesses in the market, they stopped shopping there. They were replaced by new waves of immigrants from Portugal, the Caribbean, and East Asia, changing the community and making it even more diverse.

27 OTHER TYPES OF CAMPS

When I was a child, my brain had been schooled to relate camps with places that had Nazis, barbed wire, and death. Not a place a parent would send a child. Anxiety can begin at a young age. So when I was told that we were going to a summer camp with outdoor games, swimming, and crafts, I became confused. There were other types of camps?

In 1958 and 1959, Mom took us to an overnight camp in Barrie called Mothers' and Babes' Camp. The camp was operated by the Jewish Camp Council and was geared to mothers with young children. The camp's origin goes back to 1919 when it provided convalescent care for victims of the influenza epidemic by offering a two-week holiday to mothers and young children. In 1921, with the epidemic over, the rest home was transformed from a convalescent home to a place in the country for women and children from poor families, although they continued to assist those with poor health. Mothers' and Babes' Camp continued until 1977 when the Jewish Camp Council closed it down.

As I quickly learned, there were no guards or barbed wire – just a lake, cabins, and trees. The camp had an ideal setup for young families. Each cabin accommodated two families. On each side there were two rooms, with the kids in one room and the moms in the other. During the day, we were assigned to counselors in a "cabin" with children our age just like any other summer camp. The mothers had downtime to relax and were responsible for their children again after dinner. On the weekends the dads could come up. Even though I was just five or six years old I had fond memories of the camp. We didn't return in 1960 because my sister had turned ten and the camp accepted children up to the age of nine. If she couldn't go, then none of us could go.

Fortunately, my camp experience didn't end in 1959. Irv and I were sent to Camp Northland-B'nai Brith in 1963 when Irv was old enough to attend. The camp is located on Moose Lake near Haliburton, Ontario, about a three-hour drive from Toronto. I was excited and anxious upon leaving the city for the first time without parents. The camp rented school buses to take us to camp, which left early in the morning from the Bloor Jewish Community Centre. As we got closer to the camp, the landscape changed from farmland to rolling hills. Parts of the highway had been blasted through rock formations of the Canadian Shield, and sections of the road had massive cliff walls on either side. The full school buses that took us to the camp sometimes had difficulty climbing the larger hills. You could hear buses groan and the gears grind getting to the top of some of those hills. During the last hour I found myself getting queasy. I wasn't alone. Other kids tried hard not to vomit, but that wasn't always possible. Our luggage was picked up a day or two earlier in trucks and was waiting for us at camp, all of it sorted in the main field. It was still chaotic sorting through all the duffel bags.

The camp has a long history in the Jewish community. A Jewish summer camp was first established in 1909 by several of Toronto's Jewish philanthropies, but Camp Northland didn't move to the existing Moose Lake site until 1944. It was run as a boys' camp, and girls were sent to Camp B'nai Brith on Lake Couchiching, about 90 minutes north of Toronto. The Jewish Camp Council owns 750 acres of property around Moose Lake, where Camp Northland is located. Much of the lake is camp property, and there are only about 100 cottages on the far end of the lake, so it is quiet, with few motorboats. Camp B'nai Brith moved beside Camp Northland at the Haliburton site in 1954.

When I first attended as a camper, it was bursting at the seams because of the baby boom. There were four boys' units and four girls' units. They squeezed up to 15 campers and three staff in a cabin that had poor ventilation and no electricity. Over 600 campers attended at its peak. In 1964, my second year at Northland, a satellite campsite was built on the lake and opened in 1965. It expanded capacity enough that they allowed them to reduce the number of campers per cabin. But the demand continued to grow, and in 1971 another campsite was purchased near Parry

Sound, Ontario. At its peak, the three sites of Camp Northland-B'nai Brith had over 1,000 campers plus staff in its cabins each period.

Back then there were three periods, each consisting of 20 days. The third period was the least desirable, because the weather wasn't nearly as nice in late August. The evenings and mornings were often chilly, and the lake temperature would begin to fall. Most campers chose either first or second periods. Some stayed for both. My parents couldn't afford to pay the full fees and applied for subsidies. They paid a total of $125 for the two of us. I'm sure the subsidy was also in consideration of the fact that my parents were Holocaust survivors. The catch was that we had to attend the third period. Few of my friends came for a third period, so I didn't know many campers. Still, I loved the experience – being outdoors, having cookouts, hiking, taking canoe trips, playing sports. I wasn't a good swimmer, and you needed to pass a swim test to go water skiing. I didn't pass the swim test until several years in, but I loved sports and the all-day programs, such as the color wars when the entire camp was divided into four groups. For an entire day, you competed in events and accumulated points for your team.

At the end of the period we were once again loaded onto the school buses and returned to the city, where we were dropped off at the Bloor Jewish Community Centre. The buses would pull up behind the building and we were led to the auditorium and onto the stage where parents were waiting in the audience. It was a bizarre setup and rather disorienting. In later years, the buses picked us up and dropped us off at a York University parking lot.

Most of all I enjoyed being out of the house and away from the parents, along with the tension, guilt, and boredom. It felt so liberating. Camp counselors were all about having fun, while my parents were focused on work and money. There was nothing fun about my parents. We never traveled or went on vacations, so going to camp was our equivalent to being on vacation. I returned each summer for three weeks while the rest of the summer was spent working in the family business. These were among my best memories as a child.

When I reached my early teens I stopped going to camp as a camper to earn money. For a couple of years, I landed a job at the Canadian National Exhibition (also called The Ex or CNE), an annual fair with amusement rides, a midway, exhibits, concerts, and the always popular Food Building. Someone I knew got me a job at the Shopsy's booth, which was operated by Shopsy's Delicatessen, the most popular deli in Toronto at the time. The large round CNE booth sold only corned beef sandwiches. I was a meat cutter and would work up to 11 hours a day. I would slice whole briskets, weigh the cut meat, and plop it between two slices of rye bread nonstop all day long. I reeked of corned beef. I was so turned off by the smell that I wouldn't eat a corned beef sandwich for several years after. For my first year at the CNE, I earned 95 cents an hour, which was the student minimum wage at the time. I also received a bonus for sticking it out for the entire fair. I was 16 years old with a $275 cheque in my pocket. I thought I had it made.

28 DREK FROM CALIFORNIA

My dad used a line that has stuck with me over the years. If a customer asked, for example, whether a ceramic figurine was of good quality, he always responded with a big grin, using his favorite pun, "*Drek* from California." The customer would typically think he was saying "direct from California" in his heavy accent. If the customer was to turn it upside down, they would see that it was made in China. But *drek* is Yiddish for "crap," or merchandise of poor quality. I can't tell you how often I heard that line, but it made me cringe.

My father wasn't going to make decent money working for someone else, so he eventually left Seiden Poultry to run his own business. Not to disparage my father, but he wasn't an entrepreneur. He got by for the first part of his life doing manual labor, something he took pride in. I can attribute several reasons for his lack of business acumen, but it had nothing to do with his lack of education. Some of his contemporaries – those who survived the camps and had little education – were more successful at business. They drove Cadillacs while we had a used Pontiac. But by the 1960s many survivors were middle class just as we were. Dad wasn't a risk-taker. He had no vision or interest in leaving a legacy. He was just a hard worker. That's what kept him alive all those years.

Dad also had weak language skills. I used to joke that my father spoke several languages, all of them poorly. He could neither read nor write English, which created significant barriers. As a result, any business he owned required a partner to manage the paperwork and other administrative work. Often it was my mother whose English language skills were also weak.

My father's first retail store did not venture too far from his roots – Augusta Kosher Meat and Poultry Market in Kensington Market. It was a short-lived partnership with Meir Pilc, whom he knew from before the war. Meir was born in Dabrowa Gornicza, just a few kilometers from Bedzin. Out of 11 children only Meir and four siblings survived. Within two years Dad left the business while Meir continued to operate the butcher shop for quite a few years.

In the early 1960s, my dad bought Albert's Smoke Shop, a convenience store on the corner of Queen Street East and Sumach Street. The neighborhood is now called Corktown, but back in the 1960s it was included as part of Cabbagetown. The name derived from the Irish immigrants who moved to the neighborhood beginning in the late 1840s and were said to have been so poor that they grew cabbage in their front yards. In the 1960s, Cabbagetown was considered Toronto's worst slum. In the 1970s, after Dad had sold the business and building, the neighborhood became gentrified and real estate prices took off. Young urbanites bought the Victorian rowhouses in the area and restored them.

Like many first-generation immigrants, he accepted the gruelling long hours. In addition, the ability to be perfectly fluent in English was less important in retail operations than in many fields. The store was your typical convenience store during the period, mostly selling cigarettes, chocolates and candies, soft drinks, newspapers and magazines, gift items, and some groceries.

The convenience store was open seven days a week and only closed for the Jewish High Holy Days and a few statutory holidays. My dad would leave the house at 8 a.m. and return in the evening, often after we were asleep. This was not uncommon for survivors. The hours weren't much better than when they were used as forced labor. Over time, he cut back the hours slightly. On weekends and after school, if there was no Hebrew School, my siblings and I would help in the store. It soon became our second home. Above the store was a rundown apartment with a kitchen, sofa bed, a television, and an electric hot place to heat food. If the weather was bad, Dad would sometimes stay overnight in the apartment. If our family life was dull before, it had become nonexistent.

Sometime after Dad bought the store, his friend Kalman Pilc bought the store across the street. Kalman was a pleasant, soft-spoken gentleman, which is probably the only reason the friendship survived being business rivals. At one point, they agreed to close on alternating Sundays over the summer months when business was slower. Dad would remind his regular customers to get their shopping done before the end of the week.

Mom would also work in the store, along with getting us to school, picking us up, cleaning, cooking, and everything else she did around the house. As we got older and more independent, we saw less of her. Like many children of survivors, our parents were preoccupied with financial security, leaving us to fend for ourselves. It's understandable. My dad came to Canada at the age of 40 with nothing. He had a short time frame to achieve financial security.

If we didn't go to the store with Dad, we traveled on public transit. At the age of ten, I traveled on my own by subway and trolley car. I don't believe this was unusual at the time, but I can't imagine allowing children at that age to travel without adults today. Despite this, my parents could be overprotective; in their children they saw the lives and the years they had lost during the war. Numerous people lived through me. It was a burden. And when they weren't being overprotective, they were worrying. They worried about everything. They always imagined the worst possible outcome for everything. Anxiety was pervasive in our home. They could become hysterical about every bump and bruise. I broke my nose playing football with friends but tried to hide if from them. Keeping my parents in the dark was not that difficult when they weren't around that much. My dad didn't like the idea of me participating in sports. So I never had it looked at by a doctor. I have a deviated septum and have had breathing issues ever since. If we were late coming home from somewhere, they would be waiting at the door. Yet, we were riding on public transit alone at such an early age.

At the store I would help stock the shelves, serve customers, and review deliveries to ensure they were correct. The days were long and boring, and hanging out with my dad was not fun. He was in a perpetual bad mood. What I remember most was sampling every type of chocolate bar that we carried. I'm sure that if Dad realized how many chocolate bars I ate, he would have been annoyed, but this was my compensation for having to work through my childhood.

Dad didn't have people skills. He was impatient, irritable, and distrustful. His bad attitude turned off some customers. Fortunately, customers wouldn't pick up on his biting Yiddish sarcasm. I was expected to follow people around this small store to ensure they didn't steal anything. He made rude comments about people, but always in Yiddish.

This was a poor white neighborhood, and many customers were on welfare. For a week or two before the monthly cheques were issued, customers ran out of cash, which would impact sales. Over time, the regular customers were extended credit until the welfare cheques arrived. They would bring in their cheques to the store to be cashed and to pay off their tab. I don't know the number of people were provided with this arrangement, but we were busiest in the days following the distribution of welfare payments. As a result, they purchased their day-to-day needs from us.

There were many decent customers who were in difficult situations – single moms, unskilled workers, the disabled. But there were some rough or scary customers as well. My parents were both physically assaulted by customers and subject to antisemitic slurs. As a child, I found it frightening. My father wasn't one to back down, and he once kicked someone so hard that he tore cartilage in his knee. He hobbled around for weeks.

There was an addiction problem in the neighborhood. Across the street was the Dominion Tavern, and police were frequently called to deal with disturbances. Loud drunks could be seen shouting on the street or falling asleep on the sidewalk. My dad was happy to see Dominion patrons come across the street to buy things, because in their drunken state, they were often liberal in their spending. It was a time when no alcohol was sold on Sundays, and addicts would come in to purchase multiple bottles of Aqua Velva or Listerine because they contained alcohol.

The store was robbed on several occasions, and my parents assaulted. We were fortunate that it was a time where there weren't that many guns on the streets of Toronto. The store was also broken into several times. The most common break-in involved smashing the glass in the display window and grabbing what you could. Cartons of cigarettes and cash were the primary targets. One thief broke in through a back door. Another time, someone climbed up to an upper floor to get inside. We had no alarm system, so metal bars became the best deterrent. I learned that the phone ringing late at night meant the police were calling to inform us that the store had been broken into again.

Sales were almost entirely in cash, and the biggest theft risk was walking down the block to the bank to make a deposit. Fortunately, this never happened. Over time, I learned that Dad didn't record all the sales on the cash register. A certain percentage was pocketed and not reported.

Eventually, Dad was subject to an audit conducted by the Canada Revenue Agency, which had become suspicious because he was reporting almost no income. They spent a week at the store and found nothing. They did question how he was able to maintain a home and feed a family on such little income. They questioned whether food from the store was taken home. When he acknowledged that was the case, they determined that it was taxable income and estimated an amount of taxes owing. He had essentially pulled it off.

Albert's Smoke Shop turned out to be the store he operated for the longest period. It was about 1967 when he finally sold the business. Part of my education took place in that store. It also convinced me that school was my ticket to a better life.

29 THE SOCIETY

My parents worked all the time and had no social life. They did join one club though, the Zaglembier Society, or "The Society," as they referred to it. It was a Jewish mutual benefit organization, which was formed in 1951 by Holocaust survivors from the Zaglebie Dabrowskie region of Poland. My dad's friend, Harry Ferens, with whom my dad eventually went into business, was a founder of the Zaglembier Society. Harry was its president for 25 years.

This was my parents' only social circle. Many had numbers tattooed on their arms. When I was young, I didn't understand why some survivors had tattoos and others, including my parents, did not. Eventually I learned that only Auschwitz tattooed prisoners. I remember these survivors' anguish and anger when displaying their tattoos. For this reason, I have always had a negative view of tattoo art. I understand that it's an acceptable form of expression, and that my attitude is irrational. But I can't help from associating tattoos with shame and humiliation. I have a similar reaction to cremation, which is not permitted under Judaism. Still, I associate it with my father being forced to cremate Jews murdered in the gas chambers.

The Society had regular Sunday morning breakfast meetings, which I was dragged out to on occasion. I was bored and couldn't wait to leave. Fortunately, my father was just as antsy. They also had a formal annual banquet that my parents would sometimes attend. The Toronto members were from Bedzin and the neighboring towns. The Society purchased burial plots for members and my parents are laid to rest in the Zaglembier

Society section of Bathurst Lawn Cemetery. The Society also raised money to construct a Holocaust memorial at the cemetery to honor murdered family members. The group did a lot of charitable work which was something that didn't interest my father.

These *Landsmanshaft* [mutual benefit society formed by Jewish immigrants from the same European town or region] were important to Canadian Jewish life in the first half of the 20th century. Associations of people coming from the same region proved useful in creating a safe space where immigrants could acclimate to their new country. New ones emerged – just as the Zaglembier Society did – when Holocaust survivors emigrated to Canada. The group has international connections with similar groups in Israel (World Zaglembie Society) and New York (Fraternal Order of Bendin-Sosnowicer).

As the group's founders aged and passed away, some of the members' children joined and took over running the group. Their goal was to keep the society going to honor their parents. For several years, my father paid for my membership. Being born in Canada, I had no interest in belonging to such a society and lost contact with the group. Now, in retrospect, I have some regrets.

30 MOVING UP NORTH

In 1964 we left The Annex and moved north into the suburbs, joining the Jewish families that had migrated to the Toronto suburb of North York ten years earlier. That move was made in two stages because my dad couldn't find a house that he liked in his price range after selling our first house. We moved into an apartment above a hardware store on Bathurst Street just north of Glencairn Avenue. It was a cramped, dark and small apartment, even more so than our tiny house in The Annex. We hated it. My parents were rarely home, so we were stuck in the dingy flat all day. One time we were locked out with no key and unable to reach our parents. We climbed up the exterior fire escape and I forced open a bathroom window. We only spent one year there, but it was a serious inconvenience and disruption because all three of us ended up at different schools in three consecutive school years. Not only were we constantly switching schools, but each of us were in different schools because Tamara was in high school, I was in middle school, while Irv was still in elementary school.

I began grade seven at Ledbury Park Middle School knowing no one. I was awkward, small, and a year younger than the other students, having skipped a grade several years earlier. The experience was intimidating. Walking the halls to class, I saw the vice principal pulling male students aside if their hair was too long, and female students if their skirts were too short. The Beatles and mod styles may have been popular in mid-60s society, but not at Ledbury Park. For music classes, I was placed in a vocal class rather than assigned an instrument. I have no idea why, other than I was a late enrollee to the school and that's all that was available to me. My parents were incapable of advocating on my behalf. This was a pattern for us. My parents were either clueless or useless. We had to navigate the school system and other institutions without support or guidance from our parents. I was forced to grow up too quickly. Without proper parental support, I shifted into constant survival mode and became hypervigilant. As I grew older, the roles became formally reversed, and I was expected to advocate for my parents.

That year music was a disaster for me. I cannot sing. It's fine if I'm alone in the car or the shower or in front of drunk people in a bar, but my voice was not meant to be heard in public. My mother and sister had lovely voices, but I don't seem to have inherited those genes. We would sing pieces in class, and everyone would break out laughing the moment I opened my mouth. It was one of those embarrassing moments you never forget. After several weeks, the teacher informed me that I had a free period for the rest of the year. I spent each music class in the library working on homework. It was great to get a free period, but the price was humiliating. I received a B grade for my futile effort at singing. I always wondered what I needed to have done to earn an A grade. When I left the school in June, I don't recall making a single new friend. This only reinforced my feelings of being alone in this world. I never had anyone to lean on. This was a recurring theme in my life.

During the summer of 1965, we moved again. My dad finally found a house to his liking. The house was a side-split bungalow with a master bedroom on the main floor, and two bedrooms and a bathroom above the garage. One bedroom went to my sister, so once again I had to share a bedroom with Irv. The house was built in the 1950s by Laurie Skopitz for his own family, and had upgrades and features, which appealed to my dad. At the time, I didn't appreciate what a great deal this was. We avoided the packing and unpacking along with the stress related to moving. When we were picked up at the end of our camp session, we were brought directly to the new house. The home seemed palatial compared to our previous house. The walls were white, as were the vinyl tiles in the hall, which had gold metal fleur-de-lis inlays. The basement was finished with a large recreation room with a wet bar that my parents never used. The basement also had a three-room apartment, which was likely one of the things that appealed to Dad because it could generate rent income. The most attractive feature of the house was central air conditioning. For me this was the epitome of luxury. The kitchen had a custom-built breakfast nook with a wraparound bench. The kitchen appliances were avocado green, which were in style at the time. A few years later, the stove needed to be replaced, but because green was no longer available my parents bought one in harvest gold. Although the fridge was old, my dad refused to replace it, so they went with different-colored appliances.

The decorating was garish even for the 1960s. I used to refer to it as "Jewish Provincial". The living and dining rooms were done in green and gold, with green flock wallpaper and green velvet drapes with gold tassels. These rooms were for show and were never used. The sofas were covered in plastic, which would stick to your legs if you would sit on them. We had an ugly gold pedestal coffee table with a marble top. The seats to the dining room chairs also came covered in plastic to protect them during shipping. The plastic was never removed until it finally wore thin and ripped. My dad had an interesting decorating style. If he saw a piece of furniture at someone's house that he liked, he would find out where it was purchased and buy it for our house. I realized this over time, when we would visit family and I would recognize a coffee table or chair. The pièce de résistance was the stereo console along one wall of the living room. It had oak cabinetry, the top opened on one side to reveal a record turntable, and the amplifier/tuner were located on the opposite side. There were doors located in the center on the front of the console for record storage. I referred to it as the "coffin" because to me it resembled a casket.

As gaudy as the living and dining rooms were, the main bathroom was worse. The bathroom fixtures were burgundy. And once again, when the burgundy toilet had to be replaced, the color was no longer available. So my parents purchased a bright pink toilet which fit in *so well* with the dark sink and tub. My mom used to buy pink toilet paper and fuzzy toilet seat covers to match the toilet. The same woman who bought discounted produce at the supermarket – and who would reuse the same sheet of aluminum foil numerous times – was paying a premium for colored toilet paper.

I was surprised we didn't move into Bathurst Manor, where most Holocaust survivors settled in the 1950s, including the rest of our family. I suspect it had to do with house prices in Bathurst Manor. Our house was purchased for $33,000, which was ten times as much as the first house my parents bought just a decade earlier. The neighborhood was over 50 percent Jewish, but first-generation Canadians, or greeners, were a minority. At the time of the move Irv was 10, Tamara 15, and I was 12. We had become independent enough that our parents were in the business full-time, and we were left on our own much more.

There were kids my age on the street whom I quickly got to know and hang out with. I spent time together with this crowd for the next ten years, until we headed off in different directions to attend university. Like me, they were into sports. We played ball hockey for half the year and touch football during the other half. As we got older, a couple of the guys learned to play guitar, and I was given a set of bongos for my bar mitzvah. We spent hours jamming. Eventually we became interested in girls. It was the first time that I felt part of a neighborhood and had local kids to hang out with.

Within a few weeks of moving into the new house, it was the start of the school year. Wilson Heights Junior High School became my third school in three years. Wilson Heights wasn't that much different than Ledbury Park. I think the teachers at the school would likely have problems today. Many had anger issues and could be abusive. Mr. Loader, my history teacher, was soft spoken but quick to lose his temper. When he became angry, his face would turn red and he would become violent, whipping chalk at students or kicking over desks. Mr. Skinner, my math teacher, was similar, and on more than one occasion I observed Mr. Lennart being physical with a student. It was a jarring contrast to elementary school. I doubt such behavior would be tolerated today.

31 THE FAVORITE CHILD

Parents are not supposed to have a favorite child, but research suggests that most do have one. It's most often either the oldest or youngest child. Even if a parent has a favorite, they attempt to hide it. My parents did not. I was the favorite, and my parents would frequently tell me. This made me uncomfortable because I did not want to create resentment with my siblings. From time to time, I used this information to my advantage as I got older. Mostly, in high school to leverage it for more independence.

After moving north, it was a longer commute each afternoon to attend Hebrew school. Fortunately, it was only one year until my bar mitzvah. Preparations began a year in advance. A rabbi at the Hebrew school tutored me. He suggested purchasing a recording of my Torah portion so that I could practice at home. My father took me to Hyman's Bookstore on Spadina Avenue to buy a vinyl record of a rabbi chanting my part. Back then, the only recordings available were on vinyl. Cassette tapes were just becoming mainstream, but it wasn't yet an option.

Practicing my Torah part did not help resolve my horrible voice. Chanting from the Torah is much like singing, which is where the recording came in. I played the record on the "coffin" turntable over and over until I had the tune memorized. My bad experience at middle school proved I couldn't sing. Why couldn't I just read it without the chanting? As the big day approached, I was filled with trepidation.

Since we didn't belong to a synagogue, my father had to find a place where I could be called up to read from the Torah. He arranged for my bar mitzvah at a new Conservative synagogue in the Toronto suburb of North York, Beth Radom. Many of the members were survivors from Radom, Poland who settled in Toronto after World War II.

The big event was on October 8, 1966, several weeks after my 13th birthday. People may find this hard to believe, but I was a shy child. To read in front of family, friends and other worshipers was daunting for me. Fortunately, no one laughed when I read my Torah portion, but that didn't mean I was any good. Afterwards, everyone came up to wish me a *mazel tov* [congratulations], and to compliment me on how well I did. I know they are just being kind. The most important thing is that it was over.

My dad wasn't about to spend money on a fancy evening reception. Even in the 1960s, evening receptions were the norm, although they weren't the lavish events that they are today. There was a small luncheon after services for our guests. There was no music or dancing, so the party broke up early. My suit pockets were stuffed with cards containing cash and cheques. I never saw any of the money because my dad used them to pay for the bar mitzvah. I got to keep the gifts which were mostly vinyl record albums and fountain pens. No 13-year-old has any need for fountain pens. Once we got home, Dad changed his clothes and drove down to open the store. It was a long holiday weekend with Canadian Thanksgiving that Monday, and he had lost a half-day of sales.

As the favorite child, I was fortunate. My brother didn't even get a luncheon reception. His bar mitzvah took place in April 1968, which was just 18 months before my sister's wedding. There was no way my father was going to pay for two receptions – not even a small luncheon. So, Irv was called to the Torah on his big day and then we went home. We were often told how we were always treated the same by our parents, but that wasn't the case.

In September 1967, I entered Sir Sandford Fleming Secondary School. One of the school board requirements was to have a signature of a parent on file to check against absentee notes and returned report cards. Neither of my parents could write a note in English. When I needed to bring a note to school, I would have to write my own note and my mom would sign it. This wasn't limited to school notes. If my parents were going to a wedding or bar mitzvah, I would be writing the note that went into the gift card. At the start of grade nine, I decided to fully relieve my parents of this "burden." When the signature card came home on the first day of school, I did my mother a favor and signed it for her. For the five years of high school, my mother's forged signature was on file in the school office. My parents were now fully out of the loop.

Fleming had just opened in 1964 as part of the baby boom expansion of the school system. It was an interesting time to be in school. The height of the 1960s counterculture revolution had reached Sir Sandford Fleming, and students were more politically aware, ready to challenge the status quo, and experimenting with sex and drugs. The educational establishment had mostly been conservative up until that point, which created friction with the student body. Teachers and administrators no longer disciplined students for hair length or clothing styles. Long hair, beards, and short skirts became acceptable. Several Hare Krishna members, decked out with shaved heads and saffron robes, were invited to speak to the school body. Smoking had to take place off school property. In my last year of high school, the student council negotiated a designated room where students could smoke in the school building. Back then, smoking was still accepted and about 45 percent of adults smoked as compared to 12 percent today. I remember in my first job sitting through two-hour meetings surrounded by smokers. I was thrilled when smoking was finally banned from the workplace in the 1990s.

Like many teenage boys growing up in the 1960s I became interested in girls, drugs, and music. It sounds like a cliché. I was still socially shy and awkward and didn't have many dates. Of course, dating and sex were not things talked about at home. The crowd I hung out with experimented with marijuana but that was the extent of our drug use.

I came of age during Beatlemania, and my first vinyl record was The Beatles' *Rubber Soul*. A local radio station, CHUM AM released a ranking of top 30 songs in Toronto for nearly for years. The ranking was published in a brochure format called the CHUM Chart which was distributed to record stores and music venues. We used to collect and save the charts. As much as I wanted to attend Woodstock in 1969, I was too young to travel on my own to New York state and was working at the CNE in mid-August. But I remember my first concert at Maple Leaf Gardens on December 31, 1970. It was called Winter Pops, and the performers were Johnny Winter, Rare Earth, Poco, Sha Na, The James Gang, Steel River, and Chilliwack. Advance tickets were six dollars and I sat in the upper bowl. I was blown away by the energy of the crowd and the experience of listening to live music. I was hooked.

My parents weren't home nearly enough to know what we were up to. On the weekends, they would try to stay awake when I got home in the evening. There was a semi-curfew, but I rarely followed it. Often, they would be asleep when I arrived home. When I was asked in the morning what time I got in, I would either lie or say I didn't remember. They were much stricter with my sister who was the oldest. To punish her for coming home late, Dad would sometimes lock the screen door.

My dad had some old-world beliefs when it came to women and family. My mom had little independence or say in things. She was quite creative, but he often stifled it. My father told my sister that she didn't need to attend university; she only needed to find a husband. It was my brother and I that needed a university education to support families. He also believed that as a daughter, it was Tamara's responsibility to care for him and my mother when they got old. It was this type of attitude that influenced her to get married at a young age, just a few months short of her 20th birthday.

32   DAD HATED SPORTS

There's a scene in the parody film *Airplane* (1980) that has always stuck in my mind. A flight attendant is walking down the aisle asking passengers if they would like something to read. An elderly woman stops and asks if she has anything light. The attendant responds, "How about this pamphlet, *Famous Jewish Sports Legends?*" It's a stereotype, but it also accurately reflects my father's attitude toward sports. He was never supportive of my participation in sports. In fact, he was outright opposed. He would freak out and curse in Yiddish if I ever got hurt. Anything that endangered the health and well-being of his children was a personal threat. Besides, you couldn't earn money that way. Dad had absolutely no interest in watching sports other than professional wrestling – if you could call that a sport.

I caught the running bug at a young age. For the first ten years of my life, it was as if I didn't know how to walk. I literally ran everywhere. As a camper at Northland if there was any competitive activity involving running, I was all in. Whenever there would be a running event as part of an all-day program, I would be picked to run and would invariably win. In middle school, there would be a track-and-field day in the spring, and I would win the longer races. My running career was firmly established in high school. In grade nine, our gymnastics teacher, Mr. Futa, took the class out to run four laps on the school track. Over the course of the one-mile run, I passed every classmate at least once. Mr. Futa suggested that I try out for the track team, and I readily accepted the offer.

My best event was the 800-meter race. I did well, but not good enough to qualify for the Ontario championships. No matter how hard I trained, I couldn't beat the elite athletes from Victoria Park Collegiate and Don Mills Collegiate, including future Olympians John and Paul Craig, Leighton Hope, and Brian Maxwell. We were a small school, and each year another teacher was assigned as a coach. I trained on my own, mostly because there was no formal coaching outside of track season. Working on my own was a common thread in my life. As it turns out, the top runners had professional coaching. The Craig brothers running career was supported by their father who was very involved. My dad provided no support and considered running to be *narishkeit* [foolishness]. When my daughter Sarah figure skated and played hockey, I was there to cheer her on. I wasn't going to repeat my dad's indifference to things that were important to her.

For me running was a temporary escape from the world around me. Every run presented a new challenge to push myself and to reflect on everything else going on. It was physically exhausting but mentally and emotionally recharging. In fact, it was almost addictive. A runner's high is a real thing. It's a brief and deep state of euphoria caused by the release of endorphins. It doesn't last long but it's quite intense.

At the age of 18 I decided to try a marathon. I trained on my own but had never run more than ten miles at one time. Long before charity runs such as the CIBC Run for the Cure and the Terry Fox Run, there was Oxfam Canada's Miles for Millions. Founded in the days before Canada went metric, it was this country's first sponsored walkathon. I decided to run one of their early walks, on May 1, 1971. The walk was 32 miles, beginning at the Canadian National Exhibition grounds and finishing at City Hall. My plan was to run the first 26 miles and call it a day. It was a beautiful fall day. It started at 7:30 a.m., and I took off with the other long-distance runners. I was doing great and at the two-hour mark, I had run 18 miles and felt that I could finish the distance in under three hours. Then I reached what is commonly referred to as "hitting the wall." You deplete your stored glycogen, and you become too weak and fatigued to run anymore. I was determined to continue, so I walked until I reached 26 miles and hobbled to the bus to head home. Running shoe technology was rudimentary in 1971. I had worn an old pair of shoes with broken-down cushioning. When I got home, my feet were swollen and bruised. I was in pain for two weeks.

In 1972, during my second year as a counselor at Camp Northland, I tore ligaments in my ankle, which put me in crutches. I had my first encounter with the small rural hospital in Haliburton. I had to return home early. I eventually had surgery on my ankle to stabilize the joint. It also ended any notions of being a competitive runner. I abandoned running for several years because of ankle pain. I eventually returned when the shoe technology advanced to the point where I could run pain-free. I ran for another couple of decades, eventually competing in five- and ten-kilometer runs, and even a few half marathons. But the surgically repaired ankle changed my gait. It led to knee problems and two rounds of arthroscopic surgery. At the age of 54, I was forced to retire permanently from running. Fifteen years have passed since I retired from running and still miss it.

33 RETAIL CIRCUS

Once I entered high school, I had less time for the family businesses. As I look back, the turnover rate was quite rapid. Dad bought and sold four stores in a period of five years. It was a retail circus. I can't explain why. Maybe he was struggling with his internal demons. But it could also be that he didn't enjoy retail business, even though it provided him with a good income. Certainly, it was more lucrative than manual labor.

Around the time I started attending Sir Sandford Fleming, Dad purchased Lawrence Bakery in North York. It still exists under the name Ararat. The store was in a nice neighborhood on the edge of Bedford Park and Ledbury Park. The bakery was predominantly a Middle Eastern specialty food store with imported products from that region of the world. The place was well stocked, and there was barely enough room to walk up and down the two aisles. There were large containers of imported olives and feta cheese, and the aroma from the coffee and spices was overpowering. At the time, there were few stores in the Toronto importing foods from that part of the world and it attracted customers from across the city.

The store was just ten minutes from home, and I occasionally helped on weekends. Once again, the problem was Dad's lack of people skills, and I got the impression that some customers preferred not to deal with him. Fortunately, my mother was often there. It didn't help that he had a poor understanding of the product he sold. I suspect that he likely drove people off with his approach. About two years in, one of the customers convinced my father to sell him the business.

Dad moved on to another business that was so much different. The store was called Jokeland, and it was located on Yonge Street two doors away from the historic St. Charles Tavern. The tavern has an interesting history. Above the tavern was a clock tower, which was part of Fire Hall Number Three, dating back to the 1870s. Many businesses occupied that space over the years, but when my family took over the nearby Jokeland, St. Charles Tavern was popular with Toronto's gay community. Both the St. Charles and Jokeland are gone now and have been replaced by a condominium development. The bell tower is a heritage site and has been integrated into the new building.

Jokeland was a specialty store that sold gag gifts, costumes, and pornography. Dad had gone from selling chickens, to cigarettes and candy, to Middle Eastern foods, and now porn. Because of its proximity to the gay community, a considerable portion of the porn was sold to gay people. The hardcore magazines came sealed in plastic. The store also sold illegal pornographic films under the counter. This was the late 1960s, before video tapes, DVDs, and the internet. These 8mm movies were therefore hard to come by. Police officers from the morality squad occasionally dropped in to check out the inventory, but the illegal material was kept out of sight. I was still a teen in high school helping on Saturdays, which was the busiest day of the week. To say I wasn't comfortable there would be accurate. I suspect my parents felt the same way and it wasn't too long before they sold the business. Ironically, this was the most profitable business they'd ever owned.

In the early 1970s Dad went into partnership with a friend who was also from Bedzin. Harry Ferens, president of the Zaglembier Society, was several years younger and a teenager at the time the war broke out. Harry was just old enough to be used as a forced laborer, and he survived six labor and death camps. During the war, Harry claimed to be an auto mechanic, although he was only 15 or 16 and knew nothing about automobiles. Prisoners would often claim to possess work skills to make them appear more useful. Harry was at some of the camps with my dad and was liberated from Bergen-Belsen. He remained at Bergen-Belsen when it became a Displaced Person camp. Sometime after liberation, when Dad visited the Displaced Person camp looking for family members, he ran into Harry and let him know that his younger brother, Josef Majer, had also survived the camps and was living in Konstanz. Dad returned to Konstanz on his motorcycle and reappeared with the brother. Harry was always grateful to my dad for this gesture. Josef Majer later emigrated to Israel, and unfortunately died in the War of Independence in 1949.

Harry was better educated than my father and could read and write English well. He had previously owned a grocery store, and together with my father purchased a small discount supermarket called Williams Super Discount. It was located on Queen Street East and Sherbourne Street, only a kilometer from Albert's Smoke Shop, and with a similar clientele. They carried overstocked non-perishable groceries from bankrupt businesses and regular wholesalers. This was in the days before dollar stores and no-frill grocery stores, so there wasn't much competition. Their low overhead allowed them to sell merchandise at prices below the supermarket chains.

I occasionally did the stocking and deliveries. But by this time, I was an undergrad at the University of Toronto and didn't have much spare time. The two owners stood behind the register, which became a problem. From what I recall, there was a personality clash. In addition, my father always had trust issues. I'm sure he believed his partner was dipping into the till. I'm sure he wasn't, but Dad believed everyone was trying to cheat him. Eventually, Harry Ferens bought Dad out, and he was on the move again.

Dad went full circle back to Kensington Market is the mid-1970s. Uncle Israel, his wife Dora, and their children, Helen and Joe, emigrated from Germany in the mid-1960s. Shortly after arriving in Toronto, Uncle Israel and Dora purchased Louis' Coffee Shop which was located on Baldwin Street in Kensington Market. They operated the restaurant for the next ten years, with my uncle behind the counter and my aunt in the kitchen. When they were ready to retire, my parents took over the business. It was a small diner with a counter and stools on one side, and a few tables on the other. Mom prepared breakfast and lunch items. The food was classic Jewish cuisine, the same food we ate at home. My mother also baked cakes and pastries to serve with coffee. The restaurant was supported by the Jewish merchants that still operated in the area.

After several years, they left Kensington Market, and my cousin Joe Oksenhendler managed the coffee shop. My parents didn't retire at this point. They both bounced around for a few more years, working in bakeries, caterers, and butcher shops. By the time they reached their seventies, they finally fully retired.

34 DAD'S PHILOSOPHY TO LIFE

It's hard to know whether my father's many idiosyncrasies reflect his wartime experience or whether they developed earlier in his life. As an example, his penchant for bribing officials was one of the tools he used to survive in the camps.

I observed this behavior many times in my life. It might be a government inspector or someone else who might be in the way of getting something he required. In most cases, his offer was turned down. He bribed a road test examiner to obtain his driver's license when he first arrived in Canada. He even tried bribing his own children, which he felt was more effective than appealing to their sense of duty. Prior to my sister's wedding, she had planned a trip to Montreal with her future husband. My father disapproved because he believed a respectable unmarried woman did not share a room with a man, even if they were engaged. One day he placed $50 on the kitchen table and offered it to her if she cancelled the trip. In 1968, $50 was a significant sum of money for us. She declined.

Another practice that originated in the camps and postwar years involved hiding valuables. Cash and jewelry in our home were sewn into curtains or placed in ceiling light fixtures. Our home was broken into one time while we were out. All the drawers and closets were emptied but the thieves found no valuables other than seven dollars in an envelope that I had left on my desk to pay the newspaper delivery person. Had they looked behind the dresser drawers in my parents' bedroom, they would have found some of my mother's jewelry hidden on the back ledge of the drawers. That didn't stop my dad from making an insurance claim.

My father was an endless source of embarrassment. It's one of the reasons I avoided inviting friends over when he was home. He was crude with no boundaries or filters. Had he always been like this? Was this just another manifestation of his wartime experience? I found it strange that the same man who refused to discuss sensitive events in his own life did not hesitate to act inappropriately or raise topics sensitive to others.

Some of the embarrassing moments involved taking him shopping. He would haggle over the price of everything. Once he would agree to a price, he would declare, "I no pay tax," and the haggling would resume. I would sometimes move to the far end of the store to avoid becoming involved because often the owner would turn to me as if I could convince him to be more reasonable. If it was one of his Jewish cronies, the negotiation would involve loud cursing in Yiddish. Everyone was a *ganef* [thief]. One time, I went with him to purchase a new television. He went through the usual routine of knocking down the price and then refusing to pay tax. The store owner refused to waive the sales tax. When he couldn't get his way, he turned to me and ordered, "lez go!" He marched out of the store and into his car with me scrambling to keep up. As we were pulling out of the lot, the owner ran out of the shop to stop us and sold him the television without the tax. I was forced to witness this ritual too many times and it was always a humiliating experience.

Everything was my father's business, and he had no understanding of boundaries. Dad was always commenting on a woman's weight. He would either ask, "You put on vaig?" or "You lose vaig?" And no matter how often I told him it was rude; he would continue to do it. In some cases, he would make the comment while pinching a behind.

Ever fixated on money, he would always ask: "How much you make?" I refused to tell him because it would be the equivalent of purchasing an ad in the Toronto Star and listing my salary there. Of course, he would be insulted that I wouldn't tell him. But telling my wife that she looked like she put on weight was evidently not insulting. My nephew Dov is an actor and when he was younger, he did a commercial for precooked bacon. My father wasn't impressed. He always had an opinion about choices one made in life. He told Dov that a nice Jewish boy shouldn't be in bacon commercials. Of course, he also asked Dov how much he made. Without skipping a beat, Dov said, "A year's worth of bacon."

If you bought something new, he would immediately want to know, "How much you pay?" Invariably after you told him, he would react by sucking in air through pursed lips and comment, "Oh, zo much!" In his mind, prices were forever stuck in the 1950s. His need to know was largely to satisfy himself that his children were doing well. It also provided him with something to brag about to his friends. His fixation on money never stopped. He would drop by our house, see a bowl of cherries on the counter, and immediately ask, "How much you pay?" I would tell him, and his typical response was that they were one dollar a pound cheaper at No Frills.

He was known for his crude jokes. My sister often had pet dogs, but he was not a dog lover. He would often offer to purchase from any dog owner "half a dog." This was a favorite joke, which he would repeat whenever he ran into someone he knew with a pet. He had an arsenal of crude gestures and remarks. When he disapproved of something, he would make a fist and hold his thumb between his index and middle fingers, so only the tip of his thumb would be visible. He would then declare: "This is what you get."

Dad had different ways in which to embarrass you. One of the things important to him was whether you were a *macher*. It literally translates to "maker," but means someone who is influential or a big shot. If you were a macher, then you were someone. My brother, Irv, worked in banking and my father had accounts in the bank branches where my brother worked. One time, when he was at Irv's branch to deposit some cheques, a bank vice president was visiting the branch. Another staff member introduced the executive to my father. Dad shook his hand and asked, "Who is more of a big shot, you or my son?" Fortunately, the executive laughed it off.

Money and status were important to him. One time, when I came for a visit, he told me that he was mad at me. I had never told him I was a deputy minister, the most senior executive position in a government department. What it implied was that I was hiding from him that I was a macher. I laughed and said I wasn't, but he continued to insist that someone had told him that I was. The ability to brag about his children's accomplishments was important. Dad bragged that Irv had been to dinner with the Prime Minister, Brian Mulroney. As it turns out, Irv had attended a political fundraising dinner at which Brian Mulroney was the featured guest. My father's praise was preferred over his scorn, so I told him things that he wanted to hear and kept the rest to myself. I'm sure my siblings did the same.

35 FOOD WITHIN A HOLOCAUST FAMILY

Food invokes diverse emotions and has different meanings for people. Food can be fun. Food can be comforting. Food can be connected to holidays. Food can sustain life. Food can be for celebrating. Food can be about family. Food can be about memories. Food can be about your history and traditions.

For a Holocaust family food represents all these things and more. Many survivors developed strong feelings towards food after several years of eating very little. As I mentioned, my mother traded her only pair of shoes for some food. My father spent the first part of the war in the Bedzin Ghetto where food was rationed. The final three years were spent in the concentration camp system on a starvation diet. These traumatic events shaped their future lives.

My parents wolfed down food as quickly as humanly possible. It seemed like they didn't even chew it before swallowing. It was not a pretty sight. Dad would drink boiling hot coffee and tea, throwing it down his throat. I am sure they developed this behavior as prisoners. Their meager rations at the camps were not "enjoyed." The food was simply consumed as quickly as possible before someone tried to take it away from them. Growing up, our family developed some of the same bad habit. My wife has always complained about how quickly I eat, but I can't help it. It's a bad family trait. I've since learned that this was common among Holocaust survivors. Table etiquette was not valued in the camps.

When I was young our diet was boring. Maybe that's why I became a foodie. For one thing, my parents kept a kosher home, which meant a strict set of Jewish dietary rules. No eating meat and dairy together. No pork, shellfish, or birds of prey. Mom mostly cooked what Dad liked to eat, which was not anything good. She learned to cook Polish-Jewish dishes. We ate a lot of chicken because it was inexpensive. Beef was rarely served and always overcooked. Making meat kosher involves salting it to draw out the blood, which, of course, makes the meat salty and tough. The only vegetables my dad would eat were cooked carrots and potatoes. I cannot remember having eaten anything green at home. Mom was an excellent cook and baker, and willing to learn new things, but she could only cook the same things – day after day.

Dad salted everything, whether it needed it or not. My mother used to keep a box of salt on the control panel of the stove so that it would be handy when she was cooking. One time, the box was knocked over and fell into a pot of soup. She scooped out as much salt as she could and served the soup that evening because, of course, she would never throw out food. The soup had about the same salt content as the Dead Sea. As was his custom, Dad reached for the saltshaker before even trying the soup.

"Dad, don't you want to try it first?" I asked. "Maybe it has enough salt already?"

He picked up his spoon and took a mouthful. After making a face, he grabbed the shaker again and put his normal serving of salt into the bowl.

We never ate out in a restaurant or brought in prepared food. I never saw the inside of a restaurant until I was 13 or 14 when I began to eat out with friends. My first restaurant meal was in a local burger joint called Aries, run by two Greek brothers, Nick and Spiro. We used to hang out there listening to their broken English until we were inevitably thrown out for overstaying our visit and annoying the owners. I was in university when I first went out for Chinese food. As we got older, my siblings and I introduced local foods into the house. Unlike my dad, Mom always wanted to make everyone happy. When she baked *hamantaschen* cookies for the Purim holiday, she would fill them with each person's preference – poppyseed, cherry, chocolate, and prune. When I was older, I bought my mother a wok and she made Chinese dishes, although she had never been in a Chinese restaurant. For someone who had never tasted Chinese food, she did quite well. There was nothing she wouldn't try, provided it was kosher. Before my mother worked out of the house, she made her own preserves. She would pickle baby cucumbers, make strawberry jam, and cooked pears that she bottled in mason jars and stored in the basement.

My dad was not in the least interested in trying anything new and, as I've mentioned, anything green. He would tell me: "I no eat grass." An acceptable meal for him was salted herring with a slice of buttered rye bread. He once dropped by our house after I was married, and Mary Anne made him a tea with a slice of cake. It was a zucchini loaf. He liked it and asked what kind of cake it was. I told him it was made from zucchinis. He laughed and said, "You joking mit me!" When he got home, he told my mother, who suggested that it was probably true. He immediately called to accuse us of trying to poison him. Only years later did I understand my father's aversion to green vegetables. I am convinced that it was a trigger for him. When I toured Auschwitz, it was covered with lush green fields of grass. Someone asked if the grass existed when the camp was in operation. The guide indicated that there wasn't any grass because it was eaten by the prisoners.

Other than bagels and rye bread, we didn't buy any prepared foods or baked goods. All birthday cakes were made by my mother. I didn't know about commercially baked breads like Wonder Bread until my parents owned a business where they sold it. I tried the pre-sliced bread and found it spongy and tasteless. I didn't understand how people could eat that.

Although Mom was an excellent cook, I admit that there were foods that I just wasn't going to eat. When my mother made chicken soup, she would add chicken feet, the *pupik* [gizzard], and the *helzel* [neck] to the pot. When she finished cooking the soup, Mom removed these from the pot and ate them. Nothing went to waste. She would make *schmaultz* [rendered chicken fat] and use it as a spread or for cooking. Since butter is a dairy product, schmaultz was used as a substitute when eating meat. That's what we put on our mashed potatoes. Sometimes my dad would bring home a cow's tongue, which my mother would boil before peeling off the skin and serving it for dinner. Appetizers like gefilte fish, or a poached ball of minced fish, were admittingly an acquired taste. How could I forget *flunken* [beef short ribs], which was boiled until it turned gray and stringy – just the way my dad liked it. But the absolute worst dish she prepared was *galleh*, jellied calves' feet. I used to tell my mother it looked like the scum at the bottom of the sink.

On some holidays we ate carp, which I found to be a foul-smelling, oily fish. The carp was always fresh. It was so fresh that it was still alive when Dad brought it home from Kensington Market. The fish was kept in the bathtub – our only bathtub – until it was ready to give up its life and take a place at our dinner table. It's quite the spectacle to watch a large fish swimming around while you're sitting on the toilet. I discovered later in life that other children of Jewish immigrant parents also had to share their bathtub with a future dinner entrée. There's even a children's book called *The Carp in the Bathtub*.

36 BACK TO HALIBURTON

I decided not to go back to camp for my last year of eligibility as a camper and regretted it. It turned out that I missed going to camp. Instead, I was stuck at home, working in the family businesses, and being bored. The transition from camper to staff occurs at age 16 when you enroll as counselor-in-training. The fee was equivalent to what one would pay for a camper to spend the entire summer at camp. My father wasn't going to pay that much, so I assumed my camp days were over.

When Camp Northland expanded to a third location in Parry Sound in 1971, the camp still needed staff just weeks before the start of the season. I can't remember who it was, but someone had suggested I would be interested in working as a counselor. I received a call from the camp office just days before the campers were to arrive, offering me a position. I was paid $150, which was less than what I could earn in the city, but I didn't care. I jumped at the offer and quickly packed my things. The next day I was picked up by the camp driver.

I spent the next six summers at camp, first as a counselor and later as a unit head. Being on staff was an extension of a favorite childhood experience – only better. Although the money was horrible, it got me out of the city. Since we never took any vacations, this became my annual holiday. I made a lot of friends at camp that have continued for decades.

As a counselor I would spend the day with the campers, taking them from one activity to another. Evening time was when the staff would unwind. Evenings were for socializing, which might include sitting around a campfire, playing music, or "illegal" activities such drinking, drugs, or taking a boat out onto the lake. There were always members of staff awake and hanging out well past midnight, despite the early wakeup times. In late summer, when there was sunspot activity, I would just sit by the lake at night to watch the Northern Lights. The waves of dancing lights across the night sky were spectacular.

In 1974, when I was promoted to unit head, camp life got even better. Although there were new responsibilities, I no longer stayed in a cabin with campers, but instead in head staff cabins that had electricity and bathrooms. Electricity meant a coffee maker, heaters for the cold nights, fans for the hot days, and stereos.

I felt a strong connection to camp people because many were children of Holocaust survivors. As was the case in the city, it's not something that was ever discussed. It was just the sense of belonging that existed. A driving force behind Northland-B'nai Brith was John Bernstein, a founder of the camp and the camp director. He had an unusual accent and speaking style that I quickly picked up on, and I would often imitate it – as did others. He was an accomplished individual, but by the 1970s, when I was working with him, he didn't appear to have much enthusiasm for the job. He was an avid tennis player and a constant presence in the camp in white tennis shorts.

John Bernstein had an interesting past. He was born in Russia in 1918. He and his parents fled the country shortly after the Russian revolution, settling in Paris. During World War II, John served in the French army, spent time in a German P.O.W camp before escaping, and continued to fight with the French Underground. With the end of the war, John dedicated his life to the welfare of the Jewish community. First, as a member of the occupying forces in Germany, he helped Holocaust survivors and displaced persons in Europe find their family and homes. Then, while working with United Nations Refugee Assistance, he helped many Holocaust survivors get to Palestine. Several years after the end of the war, John immigrated to Canada, where he accepted a position to work with the Jewish community in Winnipeg. He was invited to come to Toronto and direct the Jewish Camp Council during its early days and was involved in establishing Camp Northland-B'nai Brith on Moose Lake and the Mothers' and Babes' Camp near Barrie.

Camp Northland had a lasting impression on me, perhaps because it was a place to escape the real world. I continued to return periodically for alumni weekends at the end of the summer to relive those camp summers. My camp experience was put on the big screen with the release of *Meatballs,* a 1979 Canadian comedy film directed by Ivan Reitman.[1]

In the fall of 1976, I entered grad school at Temple University in Philadelphia in their health administration program. I was required to do an internship in a health care facility between first and second year. That put an end to my camp career. I was officially an adult.

---

1. The film was Bill Murray's first starring role and launched Ivan Reitman's directorial career. Filming took place at Camp White Pine on Hurricane Lake, not far from Camp Northland, in August and September of 1978. Supposedly the movie was loosely based on Northland, and the camp was even considered as a filming location. However, it was filmed at White Pine because their camp season ended two weeks before Northland's.

37 YOU NEVER CALL

My parents' guilt trips never ended. After having my own family, it became difficult to have daily contact with my parents. If I hadn't called or visited often enough. They would welcome me with, "You never call," or "You never come over." My answer would always be the same, "But I'm calling now," or "But I'm visiting now." It was constant and annoying. The problem wasn't the frequency of contact but that they were bored and needed entertainment or a distraction. In later years, calling was an exercise in frustration because they both lost a lot of their hearing. Visiting was the only viable option.

Marriage changes the dynamics of a relationship with parents. Not every parent deals with it well. If the parents don't particularly agree with the choice of a child's spouse, it can lead to years of tension. Although my parents were not pleased that Mary Anne was not Jewish, they accepted her and were happy that she chose to convert to Judaism. It helped that she wasn't the first non-Jew in the family. I'm sure their major concern was what would people say. People can be mean. I hosted a party when we were dating, and an acquaintance told Mary Anne that she looked like a pork chop at a Jewish wedding. I asked my friend who had brought this person to never bring him around again.

Mary Anne was likely the best thing that ever happened to me. At times I have felt adrift, and she functioned as my anchor. She is a person who is comfortable with lists, schedules, and routines. Whereas she has class I was short on it. I learned a lot about life from her. I was instantly attracted to her when we first met. It took three tries before she agreed to go out with me. Early on she realized that the relationship was going to have family issues and gave me an ultimatum. She told me I need to "shit or get off the pot!" I agreed and we were engaged.

As it turned out my parents were not the problem. Mary Anne's father, Frank Bonello, was quite unhappy about me. We ran into him on our first date at a Maple Leaf hockey game, and he told her afterward to get rid of me. When she refused, he threw her out of the house. This was an extremely stressful time for her and for her mother, Carol, since Mary Anne was an only child. We assumed we would be getting married without her parents present. After several months, Carol convinced her husband to back down, and we were invited to her parents' home for dinner. Her mother tried her best to make me feel comfortable. Her dad, who is not that talkative at the best of times, was like a sphinx. Over time there was a thawing out. We were married on May 14, 1981, at Beth Tzedek synagogue. Frank, who was heavily involved in hockey, was the general manager of the Toronto Marlies, a top junior team in the city. We had to choose a wedding date that didn't interfere with his hockey schedule. We had a large, beautiful wedding and my father-in-law shelled out for kosher food. However, he has always been cold towards me. I eventually accepted that this would never change. Frank was a workaholic and dedicated little time for family life. This was not the type of parent I wanted to be.

Five years later, on May 16, 1986, Sarah was born. It's one of those events that you will never forget. Mary Anne called me at work to tell me that labor was starting. I went home and had lunch. We watched a David Letterman episode that I had taped and then left for the hospital. Sarah was born at 7:10 p.m. That evening I went home and fell asleep in the bathtub. When I awoke, the water was cold. For my parents this was grandchild number five. For the Bonellos this was to be their only grandchild. She received lots of attention over the years. Sarah was a quiet, introverted child. She had few friends and was not terribly social. After she took up figure skating, Sarah would often use skating as a reason to turn down social invitations. She has always kept things to herself. I have often wondered if my parents' and my own trauma has been passed on to her.

She took an interest in skating at a very young age. At three-and-a-half she was gliding around the ice. When she spotted the older girls in their skating outfits, she was determined to be a figure skater. It was an ideal sport for an introvert because you had little interaction on the ice except for with your coaches. When she was six, she joined the York Region Skating Academy, an elite club run by Joanne McLeod, a national-level coach. Although Sarah was passionate about skating, she had neither the mental toughness nor the body shape of a competitive skater. Skaters are expected to look like ballerinas. She competed for about eight years and participated in all the club's skating shows. In the summer months of July and August, instead of going to camp, Sarah chose to practice skating. She went to competitions throughout Ontario and even to some in Buffalo. I never missed an event. I used vacation time to drive her wherever she had to skate.

When she turned 14, she pulled me aside to tell me she wanted to quit skating. I think she thought I might be disappointed. In fact, I was thrilled. I had enough of daily practices, temperamental and rude coaches, and obnoxious skater parents. Sarah decided that she wanted to play hockey. I told her that would be fine, and that I would find a house league for her. I'm not sure if it was her naiveté or the competitiveness from figure skating, but she insisted she wanted to play rep hockey.

I thought it wouldn't do her any harm to at least go to a tryout to see what it was like. We showed up that spring to a Bantam BB team tryout with the North York Storm. When signing up at the arena, she was asked what team she played for last season. She answered none. The women registering then asked which house league she had played in. Sarah answered that she had never played hockey before. The woman looked at her in disbelief but took our $20. There were dozens of girls on the ice, and I would say none could skate as well as Sarah. She certainly stood out during the skating drills, until she had to skate with a puck on her stick. To no one's surprise, she was cut. After the tryout, a father approached us to ask if she would be interested in playing down a level on a Bantam B team. He was going to try to organize a team with girls who didn't make the BB team.

That was the start of Sarah's hockey career. She had a made a rep team with zero experience. She played for several years until she suffered a concussion which scared her enough that she dropped hockey for a few years before going back to play in an adult ladies' recreational league. Her grandfather was opposed to her playing hockey, believing it was too rough for girls. I eventually invited him to come out to a game. When he realized there was no body checking in girls' hockey, he dropped his resistance.

Growing up, Sarah and Mary Anne were not close. I think they were too much alike and there was constant friction. I was forever caught in the middle. Sarah kept things to herself. Before the days of cellphones, she would have to speak to friends on our home phone. On more than one occasion, I found her speaking to someone on the phone in one of our closets. When she was dating Arthur, she one day told us she was bringing him for dinner. We never knew that this Arthur existed. Several months later they were engaged and on August 26, 2012, they were married.

Over the next six years, our family grew with the birth of two grandsons, Jordan and Zachary. I was determined to provide the boys with an involved grandparent, something I never got to experience. I have been part of their lives since birth, and it has been extremely rewarding. In the summer of 2022, Jordan, who was still just five, coauthored a picture book with me. Jordan dictated the story to me and did the illustrations. We sold over $1,000 in books, which was donated to a charity. He followed that up with a second book in 2024.

38 STRUGGLING TO MAKE SENSE OF JUDAISM

Like any young adult, I distanced myself from home when I entered university. In my case, I was also trying to create some distance from my past. I didn't want to be labeled as a second-generation Canadian with Holocaust survivor parents. I just wanted to be another Canadian. I no longer feel that way, but at the time it was important to me. I could distance myself from my past, but I couldn't exorcize it from my soul.

I was an undergraduate at the University of Toronto beginning in 1971. Commuting to school, doing assignments, studying, and social activities kept me out of the house for most of the week. In the summer of 1974, I visited Israel and my indifferences towards my family disappeared temporarily. It was an opportunity to connect with distant family members. I met my aunt Sara and her three children, as well as my two of my mother's brothers, Srul and David. Israel is a beautiful country but what had the biggest impression on me was Yad Vashem. As I wandered through the museum, I looked at each photo, trying to see if there was a family member I might recognize. I thought I recognized my father in a photo and spent considerable time trying to track down where it was taken after returning home. Eventually I realized that my dad was never at the camp where the photo was taken. That was the first instance where I felt the need to know what happened to my family.

In 1976, I finally moved out of the house to pursue graduate studies at Temple University in Philadelphia. The separation from home life was complete. I did move back for a brief time after graduation before meeting

Mary Anne in 1979. Getting married turned into a complicated process because Mary Anne decided to convert to Judaism. Planning the wedding was a challenge because the synagogue was holding the date for us but wouldn't commit until the conversion took place. That process wasn't completed until early 1981, shortly before the wedding date.

Mary Anne's conversion caused me to consider my relationship with my faith. She decided to become a Jew for me, but how committed was I? When I was young, I heard my parents question where God was during the war? These types of questions were raised when they were upset, and although I largely ignored them, they stuck in my head. During conversion classes, these thoughts would drift back into my consciousness. Where was God when children were being ripped from their mothers' arms and murdered? Where was God during the pogroms and death marches? Where was He when unspeakable horrors were inflicted on innocent people? Throughout our history, horrible things have happened to the Jewish people. The Bible states we are the chosen people. There are several interpretations of what that term means. It certainly hasn't bestowed us with any special privileges or protected us from persecution.

Whether or not God exists doesn't necessarily define me as a Jew because there are cultural and racial aspects of the Jewish people. You can be an atheist but still consider yourself a Jew. I don't think any atheist is likely to consider themselves to also be a Christian. I went to an Orthodox Hebrew school, where I mostly learned to read, write, and pray in Hebrew. Hebrew school was intended to prepare me for my bar mitzvah when I turned 13. The school taught a strict adherence to religious practice, which was a source of conflict for me because even at a young age I was interested in leading a secular life. Following my bar mitzvah, I was no longer required to attend Hebrew school, so I quit.

Yet, I have always belonged to a synagogue. After getting married, we joined Adath Israel Congregation, a conservative synagogue with about 1,500 families. It was too large and impersonal. After several years, we left and joined Congregation Darchei Noam, an egalitarian Reconstructionist synagogue where we felt more comfortable; reconstruction blends traditional practices with the modern Jewish experience. After several years, a split in the congregation developed over the tenure of the rabbi. We finally settled in at Temple Har Zion, a similarly sized Reform congregation that was closer to home.

It was an interesting progression, beginning with Orthodox congregation during my youth, to Conservatism as a young adult, and then to

Reconstructionist and Reform. Throughout this journey, the same issue gnawed away at me: was there an all-knowing and merciful God? Where was he when the Jewish people needed him? At Passover we celebrate how God brought the Jews out of Egypt where we were slaves. My dad was a slave of the Germans and was left to rot in the camps. My mom was left to starve in a ghetto in a remote part of Ukraine. As much as I try, I will never be able to reconcile my religion with the Holocaust.

39 AGING SURVIVORS

Over time, Dad did slow down, and arthritis took its toll. Eventually he walked with the aid of a cane, and later had to rely on a walker. Yet, he remained as feisty and mentally sharp as ever. Despite slowing down he remained resilient. He was struck by a car at the age of 94. While crossing the street with his walker, he was hit by an SUV driven by a woman who was distracted by her children in the backseat. He was taken by ambulance to the hospital. When this happened I was north of the city at a conference. I rushed home to find that he had already been released from the hospital. He was bruised from head to toe, but he had no broken bones or internal injuries. It was truly remarkable. He was in a belligerent mood, and his group of friends had already urged him to sue. I was working for the government on auto insurance regulations and had worked on Ontario's no-fault insurance laws. I told him immediately that he likely didn't meet the threshold to sue, but he could easily get some no-fault benefits out of the woman's insurance company for a few weeks. His response was: "What do you know?" I did contact the insurer, who was quite concerned because they assumed the worst considering my dad's age. I was prepared to set up a claim, but he was only interested in suing, so he eventually dropped the matter and never bothered even trying to claim no-fault benefits.

My father had an aversion to lining up. Later in life, he used his age as a reason to avoid lines. He would go to the bakery to buy bagels and find a lineup out the door, which is not unusual for a Jewish bakery on a Sunday morning. Dad would push his way to the front of the line, menacingly waving his cane at people and shouting, "I'm 91, I no stand in lines." He didn't care what people thought. It's as if his survival instincts kicked in. Except, this wasn't one of the camps, just Sunday morning at What A Bagel. This was a normal occurrence. My sister once took him to a fish outlet store prior to one of the Jewish holidays. The lineup snaked out the door of the store and down the street. She was about to head to the end of the line, but he darted to the store entrance and pushed his way to the front. He ignored the dirty looks directed at him, while my poor sister was mortified. I'm sure in his mind he was transported back to the camps where there were long lines for the little available food and roll calls that lasted hours before and after each day. This was just one of several of his triggers.

In the early 1990s, my parents sold their house and purchased a condominium closer to my home in Thornhill. Many of the condominiums in the area, including their building, were populated by seniors, and a good number of them were Holocaust survivors. My dad's friend Kalman Pilc and his wife Bella lived in the same building. My parents purchased a suite on the first floor, and often sat by the large windows in their kitchen with a view of the front entrance, watching people come and go. Dad joined the older men in the building, sitting in the lobby gossiping. Other than that, he had no interests or hobbies to occupy his time.

For several years, they went to Florida during the winter, but only for one month. Dad would not spend the money to escape Toronto for the entire winter. They would bring down their own food because they had no plans to eat out. This was in the days before strict airport screening. My parents would pack roasted chickens into their luggage. I swear they brought down more food than clothing.

In 1994 Dad stopped driving and gave up his license and car. I would occasionally take them grocery shopping. That was another exercise in frustration. Mom would put something in the shopping cart and my dad would remove it, muttering, *"Mir darfn es nisht"* [We don't need it]. This was partly because I would take them grocery shopping while I shopped for my own family. They shopped at discount grocery stores, and we shopped at regular grocery stores. Eventually, Dad told me he no longer needed me to take them shopping. It turned out that Tamara was more willing to take them on a tour of the various discount stores in their area to stock up on the sale items.

Parents appear to age more quickly when you don't see them every day. Without work, no outside interests, and few social contacts, my parents settled into a dull routine. Visits from children and grandchildren became the highlights of their lives. The grandchildren's relationships with my parents were, of course, different than the relationships their parents had with them. To her grandchildren, Mom was just a sweet old lady who wanted to cook for you. Dad was a kooky old guy who said funny things in his broken English. We might visit on a Sunday morning, and my father would offer my daughter Sarah some whiskey and herring or chocolate, which he referred to as "schmuckolate." The chocolate she accepted.

Aging affected my parents quite differently. My dad had no known chronic health issues other than hypertension and arthritis. He was in great general health considering his history, and he never experienced an overnight stay in the hospital until the day he died. Both my parents continued to work part time, to keep busy and to boost their retirement income. At some point, both fully withdrew from the workforce. Mom kept busy cooking, cleaning, and sewing until she began losing those skills.

40 MEMORY LOSS

My dad's health issues were minor when compared with my mother's. She developed heart valve issues later in her life, but she was not a candidate for surgery. Over time, reduced blood circulation led to oxygen deprivation to her brain, which led to vascular dementia. Initially, the signs were difficult to detect. She became forgetful, at least more so than normal. My mom was a great cook, but there was a noticeable deterioration over time. She did not cook or bake from recipes. Everything she prepared was from memory. As her dementia progressed, she would forget the amounts of ingredients, or accidently leave some out. One time, she made fried fish fillets and by mistake used baking soda instead of flour for the breading. She loved cooking for the family, but she struggled to prepare and clean up at the last holiday family dinner. We decided the next generation would host. Mom would have objected in the past, but she didn't when it was raised. Eventually even my dad was concerned. Tamara took her for an assessment with a gerontologist, who confirmed she had mild to moderate dementia.

As Mom struggled with basic tasks like cooking and cleaning, we decided it was time to provide help. Dad resisted every move. We tried ordering prepared kosher meals, but Dad canceled the service, complaining the food was worse than the food in the camps. We hired caregivers to assist Mom and do some light meal preparation and cleaning. They lasted a week before Dad fired them. "I no pay somebody to look of me," he insisted. This created a lot of stress in my life. They could no longer live independently, yet Dad was throwing up roadblocks to keeping them safe and healthy.

Mom developed blackouts and was rushed to the hospital on several occasions. My sister and I would spend long nights in the emergency room. Tamara was no longer working full time, but I was. I dragged myself into the office on several occasions on only a couple of hours of sleep. Mom's episodes were caused by low blood pressure. But on one occasion, her blackout was the result of a mini stroke which left her even more confused. We convinced Dad that Mom could not return home. My siblings and I arranged to have her moved to a retirement home. Dad refused to join her, thinking the move was temporary, but after several months of living on his own in their condo, he relented. He moved in with Mom and put their home up for sale.

He was miserable there and was complaining that the home was worse than the concentration camps. At first, I thought he was just trying to be difficult but eventually realized that the institutional setting was a trigger for him. In his mind, the retirement home was like the camps. I have since seen studies suggesting that Holocaust survivors do not fair well in institutional settings.

Three months after Mom moved into a retirement home, Dad reluctantly joined her. In August 2008, Dad asked Tamara to take him to a funeral home to pre-arrange their funerals. The day after the arrangements were finalized, he stopped eating.

It took a few weeks to realize what he was doing. Dad was 95 years old and, other than having arthritis, was in good health. Over the Labor Day weekend, my sister hosted a family barbecue. Tamara barbecued lamb, which was one of Dad's favorites. He methodically chewed on pieces of the grilled meat and then spit it out. He claimed he couldn't eat. It was both disgusting and painful to watch, but no pleading could get him to abandon his plan. This dragged on for three months during which he became progressively weaker. I kept hoping he would abandon his plan, but he stuck with it. Had they been able to remain in their condo, I am convinced that he would have lived for several more years.

It was a long weekend in early November when I received the call. My wife Mary Anne and I were away in Niagara-on-the-Lake, a town in the Ontario wine region just minutes from Niagara Falls. We were there to unwind for a couple of days at a quaint bed-and-breakfast and to visit local wineries. At work, I'd been in the middle of a major regulatory review that involved putting in many long hours, so I needed the time off.

The call from my brother, Irv, came early on the Monday morning. Dad had just passed away. He had been fading, and we all knew the end was near. Still, the call left me numb. He passed away on November 10, 2008, just 15 days short of his 96th birthday and on the 70th anniversary of *Kristallnacht* ["the Night of Broken Glass"], a day that symbolized the final shattering of Jewish existence in Germany.

Mary Anne and I went for breakfast and then packed up to return home to assist in the funeral arrangements. Even in death Dad was cheap. He pre-paid everything because he liked to be in control. When Tamara provided us with the details, I had to shake my head. Dad had rented the bare minimum number of vehicles for the trip to the cemetery, with none for clergy – a norm in the Toronto Jewish community – and no police escort. I wish Dad had been there to tell the rabbi he had to drive himself to the cemetery. We also learned that Dad purchased a basic casket with no handles for the pallbearers. I wondered how much money that saved him.

There were close to 200 people at the funeral service at Steeles Memorial Chapel, one of two Jewish funeral homes in north Toronto. The immediate family hovered around Mom to provide comfort and support although she was not the least bit distraught. The presiding clergy was Rabbi Moishe Stern from the Shaarei Tefillah Congregation. He wasn't selected by the family but was instead the rabbi of choice of the Zaglembier Society. Stern was an Orthodox rabbi, while the rest of our family was not that observant. This led to some friction between the rabbi and the rest of us. The eulogies were humorous and touching, which was fitting considering Dad's sardonic wit and cynicism. There was little mention of the Holocaust. Instead, we celebrated his life.

It was cold and damp at Bathurst Lawn cemetery. At this point my head was in a fog, and I only remember a couple of things. Mom almost tumbled on the uneven ground and nearly fell into the open grave. I was annoyed when I spotted a cousin who was smoking in the front while the graveside service was taking place. It was at this moment that it struck me that Dad's unique and remarkable life would quickly be forgotten. I don't mean because of his accomplishments, but because of his perseverance and will to live despite horrific circumstances.

Her reaction to Dad's death was not what one would have expected after almost 60 years of marriage. Her dementia had advanced sufficiently to produce personality changes. At times she burst into tears when she deemed it to be appropriate, but she did not appear to be upset; she simply enjoyed the attention she was receiving. When anyone asked how she was doing, she would respond, "I'll just have to get by without him."

She was free from Dad's control. Throughout their marriage, he resented her having any social life or independence. He had an old-world perspective on marriage, which was that her role was to serve him. When he died, it should have been a period of enlightenment for her, but her dementia ensured that it was not going to happen. She could no longer read, and conversations were awkward. We would visit on a regular basis, and our chats developed into a 20-minute loop as she quickly forgot what we had talked about earlier.

Less than a year later, Mom suffered a minor stroke that accelerated her cognitive decline. That caused a crisis within the family because the retirement home provided independent living and assisted living care, but no memory or dementia care. She needed to be moved to a facility that could better serve her needs. The ideal facility was the Baycrest Centre for Geriatric Care, which had a lengthy waiting list. Baycrest has had a long and deep connection to the Toronto Jewish community. The complex includes a geriatric hospital, a Jewish home for the aged, an assisted living residential building, and a seniors' recreational facility. We were able to expedite her admission and Mom moved in several days later.

The final year or so of her life was difficult. She became agitated and paranoid. When I visited, she often cried and accused staff of beating her and stealing from her. She would be given medication to calm her down, that also made her drowsy. She confused day and night, causing her to sleep all day and be up at night. She would get up at night and wander. Because she was unsteady on her feet, she had frequent falls. I got calls at night and would drive down to see her. She would be sobbing with a gash on her head or a bruised arm and tell me that she had been beaten by the staff. It was heartbreaking.

Gradually, she no longer recognized me. One time when I came to visit, she greeted me with: "How is Herzliya?" believing I was her brother David in Israel, who had passed away years before. On another occasion, she asked me my name. I said I was Willie. She responded that she knew someone named Willie. About two months before she passed away, Sarah and I came to visit. We were shocked to find her lucid and chatty. She recognized us and joked with us. It was a rare glimpse of the person she once was. In early March 2011, she had another fall and fractured her hip. The medical team offered to transfer her to an acute care hospital for surgery. The family quickly decided against it. She lived another two weeks. I was with her when she passed away. I have never been able to set foot into Baycrest since that day. There were too many sad memories there.

41 POLAND'S JEWISH REVIVAL

Hitler almost succeeded in making Poland Judenrein. The Germans murdered over 90 percent of Polish Jews. Most of the survivors chose not to return. They really had nothing to return to.

The POLIN Museum of the History of Polish Jews in Warsaw lists about 2,000 shtetls in Eastern Europe with over 1,400 in Poland. These used to dot the Polish landscape, and hundreds were predominantly Jewish. Most villages are still there, but with far fewer residents and no Jews. For example, my aunt Machela's ancestral home, Dzialoszyce, had 7,000 Jews at the start of the war. Today there are fewer than 900 Polish residents.

Most Polish synagogues were destroyed in the Holocaust; a mere 100 buildings are still standing. They survived the war because the Germans found a use for them, either for storage or as a stable. Some are crumbling from neglect, like the one I visited in Ksiaz Wiekli. A few have been preserved and restored to their former dignity following the end of the communist regime. A 1997 law established a mechanism by which the Jewish community in Poland could demand restitution of properties that belonged to Jews before the war, including synagogues. Restoring and maintaining synagogues requires significant resources, something that the small Jewish community doesn't necessarily possess. Therefore, the community sold some synagogues, often where there were no Jews. Synagogues were repurposed. The synagogue in Jaworzno was reconstructed after the war and is now a pub. The Hevre Café operates in the former Chevra Tehilim synagogue in Krakow's Kazimierz quarters. The

Pinczow synagogue is one of the oldest in Poland having been built during the Renaissance in 1594. It was used for storage until 1970 when the Regional Museum in Pinczow restored it. In the town of Busko-Zdroj, the former synagogue is now an electrical appliance store. The former Chelm synagogue is now a hamburger restaurant. The former Inowlidz synagogue is a grocery store.

Occasionally, outside the borders of a village, there is a small Jewish cemetery, with weeds and vegetation climbing up the shattered gravestones because there is no Jewish community to provide the upkeep. In the case in Wislica, the cemetery was destroyed with no traces of my ancestors' graves. The remaining gravestone fragments from the Pinczow Jewish cemetery were moved to the synagogue and used to build a memorial. I felt like I was visiting relics of a lost ancient civilization. The pulsing Jewish world that was here, the small shops and stalls, the bustle of people, carts, horses, the sounds of Yiddish no longer exist.

There are between 10,000-20,000 members of the Jewish community in Poland. It's difficult to come up with a number because many Poles are unaware of their Jewish heritage. Under communism, people hid their Jewish roots, and their descendants are now just becoming aware that they have some Jewish ancestry. We visited the Nozyk Synagogue, the only active synagogue in Warsaw, and met the rabbi. At one time, there were 40 synagogues in Warsaw. Of the seven surviving synagogues in Krakow, only two are still active. Many Poles are using genealogy services to trace their Jewish roots.

The cultural revival isn't limited to the Jewish community. I met numerous Poles who specialized in Jewish studies in university and are working as historians, genealogists, and tour guides. They are more knowledgeable about Judaism than some of my Jewish friends. Some can read Hebrew. We missed by a few weeks the world's largest Jewish cultural festival which is held each summer in Krakow's old Jewish quarters and organized by non-Jews. Poles fill the Auschwitz-Birkenau State Museum each week. The Kazimierz quarters have Jewish-themed restaurants catering to non-Jewish diners. In 2005, the POLIN Museum of the History of Polish Jews opened its door. It's a first-class cultural institution presenting the 1,000 years of Jewish life in Poland. People I encountered treated us well. When the topic of my memoir came up, some offered to help me with the research.

It was all very positive, but one can't ignore that Jews were now just part of Polish history and barely visible in Polish society. Whether visiting a former shtetl or a large city, I admit I didn't encounter any antisemitism. However,

I was only in Poland for 12 days, and because I was on an organized tour, there was limited contact with Poles. Poles normally encounter few Jews. There was that woman in Pinczow who turned out to be the niece of my father's first wife, Estera. When I asked the employee from the local museum who was showing us around whether it was possible to contact this woman, I was told she wouldn't talk to me. She is secretive because she doesn't want people to know that her mother was Jewish. Obviously, there is a stigma associated with Jews. Throughout history, antisemitism sometimes seems to disappear, but it will always return to the surface. Poland will be no exception.

The organizer of our trip was Jeffrey Cymbler who claimed there was no antisemitism in Poland and to prove it he wore a *kippah* the entire time we were in Poland. I never observed any reaction to his kippah. Since the end of communist rule, Poland has made some great strides to embrace their Jewish population. There has been antisemitic propaganda featured by far-right groups in recent rallies and marches.

The Polish government opposes accepting any role in the Holocaust. Auschwitz is considered by Poles to be a German concentration camp in German-occupied Poland while the Auschwitz Museum is in Poland. Poles were also victims of German aggression, but they also benefited by acquiring Jewish properties and business. Poles denounced Jews in hiding, assisted the Nazis in rounding up Jews, and operated the trains transporting Jews to the death camps. The connection of the Poles to the Holocaust is not uniformly one of complicity or innocence. Despite the threat of death, some Christian Poles helped Jews by providing them with a place to hide and by sharing their own food rations.

AFTERWORD
ANTISEMITISM, OCTOBER 7 AND HOLOCAUST DENIAL

When I awoke on October 7, 2023, the attack by Hamas in southern Israel had been underway for several hours. Tears rolled down my cheeks as I sat in horror. I witnessed a pogrom, but it was not 19th-century Russia or 20th-century Poland, but 21st-century Israel – the Jewish homeland. As I realized the magnitude of the attack and observed early footage, my mind flashed to images of the pogrom in my mother's village of Comanesti on August 2, 1940. How many others were having similar flashbacks?

Israelis quickly referred to the Hamas attack as the second Holocaust. It was the largest number of Jewish deaths in a single day since the Holocaust. A Hamas senior commander stated shortly after the raid that it was their expectations that the attack would trigger a regional uprising and the destruction of the Jewish state. Another Holocaust was clearly on their agenda and Jews considered the subsequent war as an existential threat to Israel.

As unprepared as I was for the savagery of the attack on that day, I was even less prepared to deal with the explosion of antisemitism that swept around the globe. Several weeks later, I was attending a program for descendants of Holocaust survivors. Each person commented on how they were glad that their parents were no longer around to witness what was going on. But it was apparent that those in attendance were also traumatized. As I spoke to more descendants, I learned how traumatized they were. More than one person admitted that they had arranged with non-Jewish friends to be hidden if it came to that. Another indicated that they had their bags packed in the event they needed to flee to Israel.

Israeli-Palestinian conflicts often inspire hate crimes. This felt different. The ripple effect has been outsized this time, magnified by the length and intensity of the war, the polarization of public opinion and media coverage, the spread of false and inflammatory information, and the use of inciteful language by people. The vitriol and violence spread to colleges and universities, heightening tensions between anti-Israel students and Jewish students. Jewish writers, scientists, and intellectuals were uninvited to speak at conferences. Jewish students were pulled out of schools because of the threatening environment. Jewish businesses were vandalized and boycotted. Jewish individuals have been blacklisted, organizations hosting them were hounded and venues are pressured to cancel Jewish or pro-Israel speakers, artists, films and plays.

The language used by the anti-Israel contingent was alarming. They referred to the war as genocide. Israeli leaders were called Nazis. Israelis have been called colonists. This implies that Jews have no historical connection to the land and instead barged in to take the land from the Palestinian population that lives there. But the most disturbing was "From the River to the Sea, Palestine Will Be Free." Most Jews feel this slogan, which is part of the Hamas' original charter, refers to the destruction of Israel.

As if surging antisemitism wasn't bad enough, adding insult to injury, some non-Jews arrogantly tell Jews what antisemitism is and isn't. They also earnestly insist their fierce so-called "anti-Zionism" has nothing to do with antisemitism and accuse Jews of trying to shut down criticism of Israel by labelling it antisemitic. Many critics hold Israel to uniquely harsh standards, call for its destruction and demonize its population of Zionists, which is a euphemism for Jews.

Some Jewish organizations advised Jews to "look less Jewish" when out in public, and patrols in Jewish neighborhoods increased. If you went on social media, you could thousands of posts suggesting that Hitler was right or that it was too bad he "didn't finish the job." Blaming and punishing all Jews for the actions of Israel is a new form of antisemitism dressed up as anti-Zionism. It felt so much like the 1930s had returned where it was open season to persecute, marginalize, and harass Jews.

My family's experience during the war taught me how far antisemitism could go and explains how the current rise in antisemitism has traumatized me. Nazi Germany exceeded all previous persecution in terms of depravity, terror, and death toll. It was planned, resourced, and executed with detail and precision. The Nazi German persecution started with the Nazi boycott of Jewish businesses in 1933. A similar situation has been developing since October 7, 2023, but on a more global scale.

Also in 1933, the German government enacted a series of anti-Jewish laws restricting the rights of German Jews to earn a living, to enjoy full citizenship, and to access education. The next phase was the creation of the 1935 Nuremberg Laws, which stripped German Jews of their citizenship and prohibited Jews from marrying non-Jewish Germans. By 1938, Germany had entered a new radical phase in antisemitic activity, which reached its first climax during Kristallnacht in 1938.

What is the basis of this hate for Jews? I believe it's often created by centuries-old misinformation and conspiracy theories directed at the Jewish people. Jews make up less than one percent of the Canadian population, two percent of the US population, and 0.2 percent of the world population. In many countries, including Canada, Jews are the number one target of religious hate crimes. Unlike other forms of discrimination, antisemitism is not just a social prejudice, it is a conspiracy centered on how the world operates. The Internet is rife with symbols and images associated with classic antisemitism, such as blood libel, to characterize Jews. Conspiracy "theories' – like those spread by QAnon – allege the existence of a secret society and weaponize false accusations of child trafficking and murder; these conspiracies are built on centuries-old antisemitic tropes, including claims that the fictional deep state cabal consumes the blood of children.

Demonizing or stereotyping Jews as individuals or a collective – such as the myth about a global Jewish conspiracy that controls the media, economy, government, and other societal institutions – has become commonplace. A classic example involves Hungarian-Jewish billionaire, philanthropist, and Holocaust survivor George Soros, who is widely recognized for funding progressive political and social causes. Although Soros funds anti-Israel activities, he has become a lightning rod for conservative and right-wing groups who object to his funding of liberal causes. In far-right circles worldwide, Soros's philanthropy often is recast as fodder for outsized conspiracy theories, including claims that he masterminds specific global plots or manipulates certain events to further his goals. Many of those conspiracy theories employ long-standing antisemitic myths, particularly the notion that rich and powerful Jews work behind the scenes, plotting to control countries and manipulate global events.

During the COVID-19 pandemic, the phrase "poisoning the well" re-emerged on far-right fringe platforms that blamed Jews for spreading the virus. Far-left platforms replaced the word "Jews" with "Israel" and accused the Jewish state of using the virus to hurt Palestinians or to profit off the vaccine.

Since October 7, new conspiracies appeared. One suggests that there was no attack by Hamas, but that it was staged by Israel to justify genocide in Gaza, and that the IDF killed Israeli civilians. This campaign spread despite videos and documents posted by Hamas in which they boasted about the attack. Some are suggesting that there were no hostages or sexual violence and that the alleged kidnappings are Israeli propaganda. On several occasions following October 7, age-old antisemitic tropes such as Jewish world domination have been seen at anti-Israel rallies. This parallels the conspiracy "theories" following the September 11 attacks where fringe groups claimed that the Mossad was behind the attacks and Jews working in the Twin Towers were told not to show up for work that day.

October 7 denial falls in the same realm as Holocaust denial. Over the past 70 years, a new form of antisemitism has emerged: denying or distorting the fact or scope of the genocide of the Jewish people at the hands of National Socialist Germany and its supporters and accomplices during World War II. This includes the number of Jews murdered and the existence of extermination camps and gas chambers.

Holocaust deniers claim that there was a swimming pool in Auschwitz, hence it couldn't have been an extermination camp. Indeed, there was a pool in the extermination camp; a water reservoir in Auschwitz I was converted to a swimming pool which was used for a time by the camp's staff. The existence of a pool does not refute the evidence that Auschwitz was the largest extermination camp operated by Nazi Germany, where over one million people died. Holocaust deniers will tell you that Auschwitz inmates were taught trades. Townspeople in the surrounding area saw life at Auschwitz as "luxurious," with the inmates' attractive redbrick sleeping quarters, complete with bunk beds with mattresses, flush toilets, porcelain-covered stoves for cozy heating, and double-paned casement windows. The paths were tree lined, flowers were planted before every barracks, and the Nazis regularly showed movies to the inmates. Not only that, but Auschwitz had an art museum, a library, regular concerts and sporting events, a theater for music and drama, and a brothel for lonely inmates. It also had two fine post offices because the Geneva Convention rules, strictly followed by the Germans, ensured the sending and receiving of mail by all prisoners. The kindly SS guards even provided special pre-printed cards and form letters. And their health care system was world class – after all, for the Nazis, the health of the labor force was a prime concern.

Where does all this nonsense come from? Some of it is spread by stupid gullible people who are incapable of analytical thinking. I believe much of it is produced by antisemites. Why would they spread such lies? Holocaust denial is one of several conspiracy theories directed at Jews. It is a radical form of antisemitism that denies Jews the ability to be considered victims and suggests that the Holocaust is part of a worldwide conspiracy. The revisionists claim Jews around the world knowingly fabricated evidence of their own genocide in order to extract reparations from Germany, gain world sympathy and facilitate the alleged theft of Palestinian land for the creation of Israel.

Jews react differently to antisemitism depending on their connection to the Jewish community. Although some Jews are angered and frightened by these events, others don't feel concerned at all. Some are in families with non-Jews and may no longer identify as being Jewish. History has shown that racists don't care how closely you connect with the community. They will define who is Jewish.

Jewish organizations and agencies monitor antisemitic incidents. The Anti-Defamation League found that there was an increase in antisemitic incidents in Western countries in 2023 when compared to the previous year, including a "steep" jump in incidents following the October attack on Israel. The Community Security Trust reported that Britain recorded thousands of antisemitic incidents after the outbreak of war between Israel and Hamas on October 7, making 2023 the worst year for UK antisemitism since 1984. B'nai Brith Canada reported the number of antisemitic incidents in the country more than doubled from 2022 to 2023 and reached a record high. Incidents recorded in Canada included the firebombing of a synagogue and Jewish community centre in Montreal, eggs being thrown at a Holocaust Memorial Monument in Calgary, a Jewish student being assaulted in an antisemitic attack in B.C.'s Lower Mainland and a rise in antisemitic graffiti in public places involving messages such as 'Kill the Jews" or "Go Back to Poland."

Nationalism has always worried me. Pride and love for one's country can come with intolerance and prejudice of others. I have seen it as a cover for hate and sometimes even ethnic cleansing. Elly Gotz is a Toronto-based Holocaust survivor and frequent speaker at schools. He has always encouraged students to reject hate and prejudice.

> "To hate is like taking poison, and hoping the others will die. But you are poisoned. We are poisoned. Don't spend time hating. I know we get hurt sometimes; people hurt us. People bully us. Don't waste time hating those people."

Can another Holocaust happen? I ask myself repeatedly this same question. Maybe the right question is, why can't the Holocaust happen again? Primo Levy said, "It happened so it can happen again."

Genocide is not the only concern. The 21st century has seen a trend away from democratic government towards autocracies. Democracy where the rule of law, human rights, and a free press exist provides protection to racial and religious minorities. Jews around the world need to be concerned when democracy drifts towards fascism.

Why do I mention all this? How is this relevant to this book? My family and other Jewish families that survived the Holocaust understand that these incidents are a modern-day version of antisemitism that continue to reappear throughout history. Jews have been targeted for centuries. Those who believe the persecution and murder of Jews could never happen again are wrong. It's only a matter of time. Just as our European neighbors looked away, closed their blinds, and even helped our enemies 80 years ago. What will my Canadian neighbors do should it come to that? Will anyone step in to help us? I'm not being pessimistic. This is the history of the Jewish people.

The Jewish community is one defined by memory. Long before such things as the Internet, encyclopaedias, and history books, the story of the Jewish people has mostly been passed down orally from generation to generation. Memory plays a significant role in that process. My cousin Jadzia is the last living Holocaust survivor in my family. The Holocaust survivor generation is dwindling rapidly, and they will soon totally disappear. The landscape is quickly changing. Who will be the caretakers for the Holocaust memory? What shall we remember? Who will decide if it's correct? Who will call out when the memory of those who died and survived is abused?

There is a collective responsibility for all Jews to remember. Jewish communities around the globe have built museums and memorials to preserve that memory, from Yad Vashem in Jerusalem to the United States Holocaust Memorial Museum in Washington. Every death was once a life, and their stories need to be told, because we need to honor their lives, and not their deaths. I've tried to contribute to that collective memory through this book. Not only are the survivors passing away, but so are the perpetrators, which will end the possibility for justice and vengeance. What is most important is remembering the lessons of the Nazis' rise to power. We are presently living in an era of democratic backsliding. Antisemitism is on the rise in an almost unprecedented way, both on the right and left.

Whether another Holocaust can take place isn't the issue. What we need to ask ourselves is whether things are much different than in Weimar Germany. When democracy erodes, it opens the door to antisemitism and other forms of racial hatred. The Holocaust happened because past societies failed to educate their citizens on the importance of democracy, or on how the world stands idle whenever persecution takes place. Just look at the fate of the Rohingya, the Uyghurs, and Afghan women. Elie Wiesel pointed out that although the Holocaust was a uniquely Jewish event, its implications are universal. The Jewish people will always be defined in part by Auschwitz. But that memory should not be used to foment hate, instead to prompt compassion, civility, and action. It should also not be used as a moral shield.

ACKNOWLEDGMENTS

This was a difficult book to write and so many people provided with encouragement to keep going. I wish I could name them all, but this would become the longest chapter in this memoir. I need to thank my spouse and lifelong partner Mary Anne who has supported this writing project and every other endeavor I've pursued. She endured my unavailability while I spent long hours at my computer, my emotional highs and lows, the burnouts, and writer's block.

I had several people provide feedback on my manuscript, including Tara Power, Maggie Gilewicz, Mica Scotti Kole, Benay Stein, and Cindy Heinrichs. The advice I received was a source of frustration as I struggled to find my voice, but it was the right guidance. Erica Warder helped me uncover some deeply hidden memories and gave meaning to some of my experiences.

Stanley Diamond, Jeffrey Cymbler, and Judy Golan (who I discovered was a distant relative) for their assistance in extracting family records from the JRI Poland database.

Thank you to Liesbeth Heenk of Amsterdam Publishers for giving me the opportunity to tell my family's story.

Finally, I want to thank Ellie Leonard who was my Muse, cheerleader, critique partner, therapist, a shoulder to cry on, and a friend. Whenever I would become discourage, her irrepressible optimism kept me on this journey.

PHOTOS

Zloczower family portrait, 1928. Sitting are my grandmother Tzipora, my mom, my grandfather Wolf, and my Uncle Joshua. Standing are Aunt Ruth, Uncle David, Uncle Srul, Aunt Rachel, and Aunt Mary.

Zloczower home in Comanesti in 1936.

Mom and behind her Aunt Ruth, Aunt Rachel, Uncle David, and my grandmother Tzipora, 1936.

Aunt Sara (center) at Bedzin Orphanage, 1940.

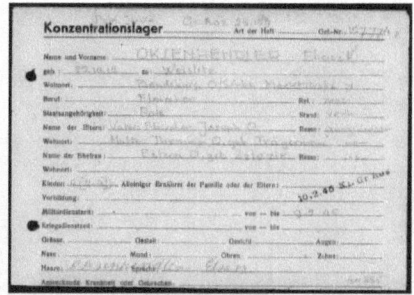

Dad's Gross-Rosen registration card, 1945.

Dad with friend Josek Secemski, 1945.

Uncle Israel at liberation from Theresienstadt, 1945.

Dad with his motorbike in Konstanz, Germany, 1946.

With Tamara and Irv and my Aunt Ruth, Aunt Rachel, Mom and Aunt Mary, 1956.

Me with Tamara and Dad. In the background is Mom with Irv, 1956.

Me, Irv, and Tamara, 1956.

On the left are my Grandmother Temerla Oksenhender with Aunt Jentla and Aunt Mariem. On the right are Estera Oksenhendler with Laja and Jenta, 1942

Mom and Dad in Israel, 1949.

Grandparents' apartment in Bedzin, 2022.

GLOSSARY

Aktion (German): Action. It refers to the mass deportation of Jews during World War II from European ghettos to concentration and extermination camps.

Aliya (Hebrew): Ascent or rise. It refers to Diaspora Jew immigrating to Israel (or Palestine prior to independence).

Appell (German): Roll calls conducted at concentration camps during which prisoners were counted.

Arbeit macht Frei (German): Work sets you free. This was posted over entrances of several concentration camps. The best known was found at Auschwitz. It was meant to motivate prisoners to work hard but the reality was that most never survived.

Ashkenazi (Hebrew): Descendent of Jews that settled in Central and Eastern Europe in the Middle Ages.

Bar mitzvah (Hebrew): The religious initiation ceremony of a Jewish boy who has reached the age of 13 and is regarded as ready to observe religious precepts and eligible to take part in public worship.

Bet Midrash (Hebrew): A place where Jews gather to study the Talmud and other religious writings.

Bris (Hebrew): A religious circumcision conducted eight days after birth by a special trained individual or rabbi.

Chametz (Hebrew): Food that is made through leavening or fermentation, and therefore prohibited during Passover and must be removed from the home.

Drek (Yiddish): Crap or merchandise of poor quality.

Dulag (German): A prisoner transit camp.

Ganef (Yiddish): A thief.

Gayle (Yiddish): "The yellow ones." It refers to Jews born and raised in North America.

Greener (Yiddish): Greenhorn, referring to immigrant Jews.

Hassidim Jews (Hebrew): A subgroup of ultra-observant Jews that originated in Eastern Europe in the 18th century.

Judenrat (German): An administrative body established in German-occupied Europe during World War II to represent the Jewish community in dealings with Nazi authorities. Also referred to as a Jewish Council.

Judenrein (German): Also referred to as *Judenfrei*. Translates to cleansed of Jews. A label used by Nazi authorities during the Holocaust for a region that no longer had Jews residing there.

Kaddish (Hebrew): Also known as the Mourner's Prayer, it is said to honor the memory of a person after their passing. It can be recited for the first 11 months following a death, and on the anniversary of the deceased's passing.

Kapo (German): A prisoner in a Nazi camp who was assigned by the SS guards to supervise forced labor or carry out administrative tasks.

Kosher (Hebrew): Food that meets Jewish dietary laws and is therefore permitted to be eaten.

Kristallnacht (German): Night of broken glass. It refers to a pogrom against Jews carried out by the Nazi Party throughout Nazi Germany on November 9-10, 1938. It comes from the shards of broken glass that littered the streets after the windows of Jewish-owned stores were broken.

Landsmanshaft (Yiddish): Mutual benefit society formed by Jewish immigrants from the same European town or region.

Macher (Yiddish): It translates to maker. It refers to someone who is influential or important.

Mal'ach Ha'Mavet (Hebrew): It translates to the Angel of Death. It was the name used by the prisoners at Auschwitz-Birkenau concentration camp for Josef Mengle who was a member of the team of doctors who selected victims to be murdered in the gas chambers.

Mikvah (Hebrew): A ritual bath used by observant married Jewish women. They are required to immerse themselves once a month after their menstrual cycle.

Matzah (Hebrew): Unleavened flatbread that is part of Jewish cuisine and forms an integral element of the Passover festival, during which bread and other grain products are forbidden.

Pogrom (Russian): A violent riot incited with the aim of massacring or expelling an ethnic or religious group, particularly Jews. They occurred in Eastern Europe during the 19th and 20th centuries.

Rosh Hashanah (Hebrew): Jewish New Year,

Seder (Hebrew): Ritual feast at the beginning of the Jewish holiday of Passover.

Shamas (Hebrew): A person who assists in the running of synagogue services and may be responsible for the synagogue's day-to-day functioning.

Shoah (Hebrew): The Hebrew name for the Holocaust.

Shochet (Hebrew): A person who is trained to slaughter animals according to the Jewish dietary laws.

Shtetls (Yiddish): Small communities that were predominantly inhabited by Jews in Eastern Europe until the Holocaust.

Schutzstaffel or SS (German): A major paramilitary organization under Adolf Hitler and the Nazi Party. The SS had three major components. One was responsible for enforcing the racial policy of Nazi Germany. Another consisted of the combat units. A third component ran the concentration camps and extermination camps.

Shtiebel (Yiddish): A place used for communal Jewish prayer outside of a formal synagogue. It is typically as small as a room in a private home or a place of business which is set aside for the express purpose of prayer.

Shul (Yiddish): A synagogue or house of prayer.

Sonderkommando (German): A special work unit in a concentration camp or extermination camp composed of prisoners, usually Jews, who were forced, on threat of their own deaths, to aid with the disposal of gas chamber victims during the Holocaust.

Torah (Hebrew): It is the compilation of the first five books of the Hebrew Bible. Traditionally, the words of the Torah are written on a scroll by a scribe in Hebrew.

Vishnik (Yiddish): Homemade cherry brandy adapted from the Romanians who call it visinata.

Yom Kippur (Hebrew): The Day of Atonement. It is the holiest day in Judaism, primarily centered on fasting, atonement and repentance.

ABOUT THE AUTHOR

Willie Handler has reinvented himself on several occasions throughout his work career. He has been a hospital administrator, a government policy manager, an insurance expert, and consultant.

Following his retirement from the Ontario public service, Willie began a writing career. He has published three fiction novels and numerous journal articles over the past few years. He is a member of the Canadian Authors Association, Writing Community of York Region, Toronto Chapter of Sisters in Crime, and the Stephen Leacock Association. His memoir *Out From the Shadows* is his first non-fiction publication. He is currently working on a book that deals with intergenerational trauma in descendants of Holocaust survivors.

Willie is active in Toronto's Holocaust second generation and third generation survivor community, participating in educational programs, commemorative events, and group discussions. He is also a volunteer at the Toronto Holocaust Museum, where he assists students and visitors as they make their way through the museum's gallery. Willie has spoken online and at in-person events on the Holocaust and his family's experience.

BIBLIOGRAPHY

Butnaru, I.C. and Spodheim, Renee. *The Silent Holocaust: Romania and Its Jews*. Greenwood Press, 1992.

Canadian Museum of Immigration at Pier 21. Web. Retrieved from https://pier21.ca/research/immigration-records/ship-arrival-search.

Carmelly, Felicia. *Across the Rivers of Memory*. Azrieli Foundation: Toronto, 2015.

Eger, Dr. Edith Eva. *The Choice*. Scribner: New York, 2017.

Eisen, Max. *By Chance Alone*. HarperCollins Publishing: Toronto, 2016.

Eisenstein, Bernice. *I Was a Child of Holocaust Survivors*. McLellan & Stewart: Toronto, 2006.

Epstein, Helen. *Children of the Holocaust*. Penguin Books: New York, 1988.

Frankl, Viktor E. *Man's Search for Meaning*. Beacon Press: Boston, 1959.

International Commission on the Holocaust in Romania. "Final Report." 2004.

Fulbrook, Mary. *A Small Town Near Auschwitz*. Oxford University Press, 2012.

"GrossRosen Concentration Camp – Stories." Retrieved from https://www.fold3.com/page/286060914/gross-rosen-concentration-camp/stories.

Ioanid, Radu. *The Holocaust in Romania: The Destruction of Jews and Gypsies Under the Antonescu Regime, 1940-1944*. Ivan R. Dee: Chicago, 2008.

Jarzombek, Mark. *From Bedzin to Blechhammer to Buchenwald: The Survival Story of Henry and Mathias Jarzombek*. Library Digital Collection of the United States Holocaust Memorial Museum, 2019.

Klein, Ruth. *Surviving the Survivors*. She Writes Press, 2018.

Laskier, Rutka. Rutka's Notebook: January-April 1943, Jerusalem, Yad Vashem. Ontario Jewish Archives: Louis Tepperman collection, 2007. Web.

Laytner, Mel. *What They Didn't Burn: Uncovering My Father's Holocaust Secrets*. Sparkpress, 2021.

Lederman, Marsha. *Kiss the Red Stairs*. McLelland & Stewart, 2022.

Paldiel, Mordecai. *Polish Heroism during World War II*. Jewish Journal, 2021.

Ploscarius, Iemima D. "Institutions for survival: The Shargorod ghetto during the Holocaust in Romanian Transnistria." Cambridge University Press, 2018. Web.

RMS Scythia Passenger List: 20 March 1953. Web. Retrieved from https://www.gjenvick.com/Passengers/Cunard/Scythia-PassengerList-1953-03-20.html.

Rosenblatt, Mira and Rosenbalt Levani, Belinda. Strength: My Memoir. Memoirs Plus: New York, 2020.

Sacks, John. *An Eye or an Eye*. HarperCollins: New York, 1993.

Sismondo, Christine. "History's lessons on dealing with Canada's neo-Nazi groups." Maclean's Magazine, 2017.

The Global Home for Jewish Genealogy. https://www.jewishgen.org/.

United States Holocaust Memorial Museum. https://www.ushmm.org/.

United States Holocaust Memorial Museum Encyclopedia of Camps and Ghettos, 1933-1945: Volume 1, Indiana University Press, 2009.

United States Holocaust Memorial Museum Encyclopedia of Camps and Ghettos, 1933-1945: Volume 11, Indiana University Press, 2012.

Weiss, Ann. *The Last Album: Eyes From The Ashes Of Auschwitz-Birkenau*. W.W. Norton & Company, 2001.

AMSTERDAM PUBLISHERS
HOLOCAUST LIBRARY

The series **Holocaust Survivor Memoirs World War II** consists of the following autobiographies of survivors:

Outcry. Holocaust Memoirs, by Manny Steinberg

Hank Brodt Holocaust Memoirs. A Candle and a Promise, by Deborah Donnelly

The Dead Years. Holocaust Memoirs, by Joseph Schupack

Rescued from the Ashes. The Diary of Leokadia Schmidt, Survivor of the Warsaw Ghetto, by Leokadia Schmidt

My Lvov. Holocaust Memoir of a twelve-year-old Girl, by Janina Hescheles

Remembering Ravensbrück. From Holocaust to Healing, by Natalie Hess

Wolf. A Story of Hate, by Zeev Scheinwald with Ella Scheinwald

Save my Children. An Astonishing Tale of Survival and its Unlikely Hero, by Leon Kleiner with Edwin Stepp

Holocaust Memoirs of a Bergen-Belsen Survivor & Classmate of Anne Frank, by Nanette Blitz Konig

Defiant German - Defiant Jew. A Holocaust Memoir from inside the Third Reich, by Walter Leopold with Les Leopold

In a Land of Forest and Darkness. The Holocaust Story of two Jewish Partisans, by Sara Lustigman Omelinski

Holocaust Memories. Annihilation and Survival in Slovakia, by Paul Davidovits

From Auschwitz with Love. The Inspiring Memoir of Two Sisters' Survival, Devotion and Triumph Told by Manci Grunberger Beran & Ruth Grunberger Mermelstein, by Daniel Seymour

Remetz. Resistance Fighter and Survivor of the Warsaw Ghetto, by Jan Yohay Remetz

My March Through Hell. A Young Girl's Terrifying Journey to Survival, by Halina Kleiner with Edwin Stepp

Roman's Journey, by Roman Halter

Beyond Borders. Escaping the Holocaust and Fighting the Nazis. 1938-1948, by Rudi Haymann

The Engineers. A memoir of survival through World War II in Poland and Hungary, by Henry Reiss

Spark of Hope. An Autobiography, by Luba Wrobel Goldberg

Footnote to History. From Hungary to America. The Memoir of a Holocaust Survivor, by Andrew Laszlo

The Courtyard. A memoir, by Ben Parket with Alexa Morris

Run, Mendel Run, by Milton H. Schwartz

The series **Holocaust Survivor True Stories**
consists of the following biographies:

Among the Reeds. The true story of how a family survived the Holocaust, by Tammy Bottner

A Holocaust Memoir of Love & Resilience. Mama's Survival from Lithuania to America, by Ettie Zilber

Living among the Dead. My Grandmother's Holocaust Survival Story of Love and Strength, by Adena Bernstein Astrowsky

Heart Songs. A Holocaust Memoir, by Barbara Gilford

Shoes of the Shoah. The Tomorrow of Yesterday, by Dorothy Pierce

Hidden in Berlin. A Holocaust Memoir, by Evelyn Joseph Grossman

Separated Together. The Incredible True WWII Story of Soulmates Stranded an Ocean Apart, by Kenneth P. Price, Ph.D.

The Man Across the River. The incredible story of one man's will to survive the Holocaust, by Zvi Wiesenfeld

If Anyone Calls, Tell Them I Died. A Memoir, by Emanuel (Manu) Rosen

The House on Thrömerstrasse. A Story of Rebirth and Renewal in the Wake of the Holocaust, by Ron Vincent

Dancing with my Father. His hidden past. Her quest for truth. How Nazi Vienna shaped a family's identity, by Jo Sorochinsky

The Story Keeper. Weaving the Threads of Time and Memory - A Memoir, by Fred Feldman

Krisia's Silence. The Girl who was not on Schindler's List, by Ronny Hein

Defying Death on the Danube. A Holocaust Survival Story, by Debbie J. Callahan with Henry Stern

A Doorway to Heroism. A decorated German-Jewish Soldier who became an American Hero, by W.Jack Romberg

The Shoemaker's Son. The Life of a Holocaust Resister, by Laura Beth Bakst

The Redhead of Auschwitz. A True Story, by Nechama Birnbaum

Land of Many Bridges. My Father's Story, by Bela Ruth Samuel Tenenholtz

Creating Beauty from the Abyss. The Amazing Story of Sam Herciger, Auschwitz Survivor and Artist, by Lesley Ann Richardson

On Sunny Days We Sang. A Holocaust Story of Survival and Resilience, by Jeannette Grunhaus de Gelman

Painful Joy. A Holocaust Family Memoir, by Max J. Friedman

I Give You My Heart. A True Story of Courage and Survival, by Wendy Holden

In the Time of Madmen, by Mark A. Prelas

Monsters and Miracles. Horror, Heroes and the Holocaust, by Ira Wesley Kitmacher

Flower of Vlora. Growing up Jewish in Communist Albania, by Anna Kohen

Aftermath: Coming of Age on Three Continents. A Memoir, by Annette Libeskind Berkovits

Not a real Enemy. The True Story of a Hungarian Jewish Man's Fight for Freedom, by Robert Wolf

Zaidy's War. Four Armies, Three Continents, Two Brothers. One Man's Impossible Story of Endurance, by Martin Bodek

The Glassmaker's Son. Looking for the World my Father left behind in Nazi Germany, by Peter Kupfer

The Apprentice of Buchenwald. The True Story of the Teenage Boy Who Sabotaged Hitler's War Machine, by Oren Schneider

Good for a Single Journey, by Helen Joyce

Burying the Ghosts. She escaped Nazi Germany only to have her life torn apart by the woman she saved from the camps: her mother, by Sonia Case

American Wolf. From Nazi Refugee to American Spy. A True Story, by Audrey Birnbaum

Bipolar Refugee. A Saga of Survival and Resilience, by Peter Wiesner

In the Wake of Madness. My Family's Escape from the Nazis, by Bettie Lennett Denny

Before the Beginning and After the End, by Hymie Anisman

I Will Give Them an Everlasting Name. Jacksonville's Stories of the Holocaust, by Samuel Cox

Hiding in Holland. A Resistance Memoir, by Shulamit Reinharz

The Ghosts on the Wall. A Grandson's Memoir of the Holocaust, by Kenneth D. Wald

The series **Jewish Children in the Holocaust** consists of the following autobiographies of Jewish children hidden during WWII in the Netherlands:

Searching for Home. The Impact of WWII on a Hidden Child, by Joseph Gosler

Sounds from Silence. Reflections of a Child Holocaust Survivor, Psychiatrist and Teacher, by Robert Krell

Sabine's Odyssey. A Hidden Child and her Dutch Rescuers, by Agnes Schipper

The Journey of a Hidden Child, by Harry Pila and Robin Black

The series **New Jewish Fiction** consists of the following novels, written by Jewish authors. All novels are set in the time during or after the Holocaust.

The Corset Maker. A Novel, by Annette Libeskind Berkovits

Escaping the Whale. The Holocaust is over. But is it ever over for the next generation? by Ruth Rotkowitz

When the Music Stopped. Willy Rosen's Holocaust, by Casey Hayes

Hands of Gold. One Man's Quest to Find the Silver Lining in Misfortune, by Roni Robbins

The Girl Who Counted Numbers. A Novel, by Roslyn Bernstein

There was a garden in Nuremberg. A Novel, by Navina Michal Clemerson

The Butterfly and the Axe, by Omer Bartov

To Live Another Day. A Novel, by Elizabeth Rosenberg

A Worthy Life. Based on a True Story, by Dahlia Moore

The Right to Happiness. After all they went through. Stories, by Helen Schary Motro

To Love Another Day. A Novel, by Elizabeth Rosenberg

The series **Holocaust Heritage** consists of the following memoirs by 2G:

The Cello Still Sings. A Generational Story of the Holocaust and of the Transformative Power of Music, by Janet Horvath

The Fire and the Bonfire. A Journey into Memory, by Ardyn Halter

The Silk Factory: Finding Threads of My Family's True Holocaust Story, by Michael Hickins

Winter Light. The Memoir of a Child of Holocaust Survivors, by Grace Feuerverger

Out from the Shadows. Growing up with Holocaust Survivor Parents, by Willie Handler

Stumbling Stones, by Joanna Rosenthall

The Unspeakable. Breaking decades of family silence surrounding the Holocaust, by Nicola Hanefeld

Hidden in Plain Sight. A Journey into Memory and Place, by Julie Brill

Untold. From Austria to America and Back, by Anne Hand

The series **Holocaust Books for Young Adults** consists of the following novels, based on true stories:

The Boy behind the Door. How Salomon Kool Escaped the Nazis. Inspired by a True Story, by David Tabatsky

Running for Shelter. A True Story, by Suzette Sheft

The Precious Few. An Inspirational Saga of Courage based on True Stories, by David Twain with Art Twain

Dark Shadows Hover, by Jordan Steven Sher

The Sun will Shine on You again one Day, by Cynthia Monsour

The series **WWII Historical Fiction** consists of the following novels, some of which are based on true stories:

Mendelevski's Box. A Heartwarming and Heartbreaking Jewish Survivor's Story, by Roger Swindells

A Quiet Genocide. The Untold Holocaust of Disabled Children in WWII Germany, by Glenn Bryant

The Knife-Edge Path, by Patrick T. Leahy

Brave Face. The Inspiring WWII Memoir of a Dutch/German Child, by I. Caroline Crocker and Meta A. Evenbly

When We Had Wings. The Gripping Story of an Orphan in Janusz Korczak's Orphanage. A Historical Novel, by Tami Shem-Tov

Jacob's Courage. Romance and Survival amidst the Horrors of War, by Charles S. Weinblatt

A Semblance of Justice. Based on true Holocaust experiences, by Wolf Holles

Under the Pink Triangle, by Katie Moore

Amsterdam Publishers Newsletter

Subscribe to our Newsletter by selecting the menu at the top (right) of **amsterdampublishers.com** or scan the QR-code below.

Receive a variety of content such as:

- A welcome message by the founder
- Free Holocaust memoirs
- Book recommendations
- News about upcoming releases
- Chance to become an AP Reviewer.

www.ingramcontent.com/pod-product-compliance
Lightning Source LLC
LaVergne TN
LVHW041928070526
838199LV00051BA/2743